KU-722-520

The Social Psychology of
Childhood Disability

The Social Psychology of Childhood Disability

DAVID THOMAS

Methuen & Co Ltd

First published in 1978
by Methuen & Co Ltd
11 New Fetter Lane, London EC4P 4EE
© 1978 David Thomas

Printed in Great Britain at the
University Press, Cambridge

ISBN 0 416 80840 9 (hardbound)
ISBN 0 416 80850 6 (paperback)

This title is available in both hardbound
and paperback editions. The paperback
edition is sold subject to the condition that
it shall not, by way of trade or otherwise, be
lent, resold, hired or otherwise circulated
without the publisher's prior consent in any
form of binding or cover other than that in
which it is published and without a similar
condition including this condition being
imposed on the subsequent purchaser.

Contents

Preface

Those who work with handicapped children tend to have a concern for particular groups or categories of children, such as the physically handicapped or the deaf. This is a reflection on the way we have classified such children, grouping those with similar handicaps together through common institutional provision. To some extent this rather rigid demarcation of professional interest is weakening, and teachers, social workers, physiotherapists and others are obliged to know something about a wide range of disorders and disabilities in childhood. I hope the reader will find something of interest here, both with regard to specific concerns and in adjacent and allied areas.

Some years ago I read the phrase 'the spontaneous revulsion to the deformed'. The phrase seemed to be both potent and provocative. Was there a spontaneous revulsion to disabilities in children, or did such conditions evoke a more compassionate response? If there was this negative reaction, was it not possible to explain it more accurately by reference to social conditioning rather than to biology? How were those who were reacted to in this manner affected, and why were there some people who actively sought contact with those who were supposed to excite instinctive hostile reactions?

In assembling materials related to social behaviour and handicaps in childhood it became apparent that not all handicapping conditions had proved equally interesting to research workers. Nor is it surprising that in an area dominated by medical and educational approaches, the available insights on social behaviour and social interactions are at an impressionistic rather than at an objective stage.

Since the study of the social behaviour and social experiences of handicapped children is still at an early stage, the material to construct even a temporary structure has to be gathered from what is to hand. At this stage it seemed to me worthwhile to discover what was known or believed, and to evaluate it in the light of experience rather than to exhaustively catalogue imperfections of research design, sampling or methodology. Therefore we need to treat these impressions as open to debate, dispute and investigation. Even with evidence of an unimpeachable character there can be difficulties in interpreting evidence collected at some time in the past, since each generation of children are influenced by the attitudes which surround their growth and development and those attitudes are themselves subject to substantial revision and change. There is no doubt that the next generation of handicapped children will grow up in a world expressing markedly different attitudes towards them, compared even to those experienced by the present cohort.

I have not used the term 'exceptional children', which is in popular usage, especially in the United States where it includes the outstandingly talented or intellectually gifted child. Since I have not been concerned with this last group, there seemed to be no valid reason to use the expression, although it has considerable appeal as a general term. Again, there are problems associated with general terms such as 'handicap' and 'disability'; however, while they can quite properly be differentiated, I have decided to follow popular usage in this instance and have used them interchangeably.

1 Social psychology and handicap

What is social psychology?

A glance at the contents list in a basic reference work — for example, Lindzey and Aronson's *The Handbook of Social Psychology* — gives a general idea of the concerns of the social psychologist. We see that the subject is old enough to have an historical framework (most textbooks nod deferentially towards Aristotle), several major theoretical positions, a richness of research methods and a variety of applied fields. Within these broad divisions we find such topics as theories of human behaviour, roles and attitude changes, person perception (the manner in which we appraise and judge others), group leadership, socialization, social structure and so on. Almost as varied as the topics are the methods of investigation, which include observation, participant observation, interviews, attitude measurement, simulation, and what some would regard as the main technique, experiment. These and other methods are applied to specific areas — industrial social psychology, cross-cultural research, the social psychology of education, religion, politics, economics, international affairs, mental health, ethnic relationships and the media.

A natural question is: can these various concerns have anything in common? Or is social psychology, as some have suggested, just an ill-defined territory which those calling themselves social psychologists have claimed as their preserve? It is a broad and diverse field with imprecise boundaries and an uneasy relationship with the parent disciplines of sociology and psychology. Nevertheless, there is a valid if somewhat tenuous unity — a concern for human behaviour in a social context. 'It [social psychology] deals with man as a social animal and investigates how he thinks, feels and behaves in social situations' (Freedman, Carlsmith and Sears, 1970, p.vii). A recent historical survey of social psychology provided several definitions (Sahakian, 1974):

> the study of individual behaviour as a function of social stimuli; the scientific study of the experiences and behaviour of individuals in relation to social-stimuli situations; the study of the thoughts, feelings and behaviour of individuals and how they are influenced by others; the perceptions of others and groups of others; the study of attitudes and attitude change.

Though there are differences in emphasis, these definitions illustrate that social psychology is an attempt to study objectively and systematically man's responses to and effects upon his social environment. This includes observable public behaviour as well as private opinions, beliefs and attitudes; responses and reactions in encounters with other individuals; behaviour in small groups or large organizations or in crowds. Given such a broad interest, social psychology cannot be accused of being modest in its territorial claims, but perhaps it is this very breadth and the central concern for human beings reacting to and influencing others that make the subject an absorbing one. It might be helpful here to illustrate, just briefly, some of the topics which engage social psychologists, particularly in the area of personal interaction.

(1) We form impressions of other people when we meet them. We do this quite quickly and often on the basis of limited information. Which 'bits' of information do we use and which are the most important? Is it age or sex, race or nationality, appearance, voice, manner? A related question is whether we are consistent in our appraisal of others or, as seems likely, are we influenced by our moods? And, further, to what extent does our impression of other persons depend on our relationship to them? Will our judgement be affected if we learn that someone has the power to make life more pleasant or unpleasant for us? In one experiment two groups of young men were shown

the same set of photographs of serving officers. One group was about to be conscripted, the other was not. The first group rated the officers as more threatening and as of greater military ability than did the second group.

(2) If we know or believe that a person has a given attribute, are we likely to believe that he has certain others as well? Is someone who is 'highly intelligent' seen as possessing other qualities, such as imagination, consideration or reliability? In one study, people who were believed to be 'inconsiderate' were also judged irritable, boastful, cold and hypercritical — without any supporting evidence for these traits.

(3) A deceptively simple question is: whom do we like? Do we like those who are similar to us — and what does 'similar' mean? Does it refer to age, sex, social class, education, occupation, or values and attitudes? Many studies have shown that proximity is enough to initiate a liking for someone, but for sustained friendship similar values and attitudes may be necessary. One study investigated the pattern of friendship among dwellers in an apartment block. They were asked about other residents in the block whom they saw socially, and the replies showed that most people formed friendships with those living nearest to them.

(4) Perhaps an important element in liking or disliking other persons is what they say about us. In one experiment subjects heard a confederate of the investigator making either positive or negative statements about them. Generally the subjects reciprocated the confederate's evaluation. A variant was to have the confederate initially make negative statements and then gradually make more and more positive ones. Here subjects reported *greater* liking for the confederate than when he made only positive statements. The original negative comments had aroused anxiety, doubts and irritation, and the subsequent positive remarks were not only rewarding in themselves, but were enhanced because they reduced the feelings aroused by the negative ones.

(5) One characteristic of groups of people is that they will some-times act collectively in ways in which they would not act individually. Within a group, especially a large group such as a crowd, we give up part of our individuality. On our own we

are personally responsible, but as members of a group we share responsibility for our actions. For example, in an experiment a group of girls were greeted by name, wore name tags and were easily identifiable as individuals. Later the girls wore concealing lab coats and hoods and were not identified by name. In both cases the girl were invited to give 'electric shocks' to a girl not in the group, and they gave almost twice as many shocks when they were part of the anonymous crowd.

These illustrations point up some of the questions that psychology asks about everyday interpersonal behaviour — impression formation, liking, attitudes, social learning, group behaviour, and the effects of stress and anxiety.

Social psychology and the handicapped

Obviously many of the issues touched upon above are directly relevant to the handicapped person's role, status and behaviour in society. Topics such as interpersonal behaviour, attitudes, impression formation, liking, etc., are ones which will concern us, and especially those facets of behaviour which influence child development.

A disability is the lack or loss of a function or a capacity. In a sense this is an objective limitation imposed by disease or accident (of life or birth). The term 'handicap' is sometimes synonymous with disability but has certain psychological overtones. Whether a disability becomes a handicap depends on its nature and severity, its prognosis and amenability to treatment, the extent to which it interferes with everyday life, and the attitudes of other people to it. The extent to which a disability is a handicap also depends on the personal meaning the loss of function has for an individual. Those with experience of the disabled will readily call to mind persons who have been able to reduce the handicapping effect of their disability to a minimum, whilst others, similarly affected, have been submerged by it. While the distinction between disability and handicap is worthy of note, in practice the terms have become interchangeable and are used in this way here.

We have seen that social psychology is concerned with man as a social animal, how he thinks, feels and behaves in social situations.

We can, therefore, ask whether behaviour, feelings and thoughts are changed if one is disabled or handicapped, or if one is interacting with a person so afflicted. A whole host of questions arise. What is the general attitude to disability? Are attitudes changing — if so, why, and how fast or slowly and in what direction? Are there different attitudes towards disabled children and disabled adults? Are there distinctive attitudes to particular kinds of disability, for instance to congenital as against acquired afflictions? How do the disabled view the rest of us and our attitudes? What is the social status of the disabled — do they have equal opportunities in education and employment? What is the impact of a handicapped child on the family? We shall explore some of these issues as they affect children and those who live and work with them.

In Britain there are between one-and-a-half and three million adults who are disabled in some way. To add those who are under 16 years of age would inflate the total figure to somewhere near 6 per cent of the population (Townsend, 1973). This includes those maimed in war, victims of industrial and traffic accidents, and those affected by illness or disease. The disabled population is wide in age range, and in the severity and causes of disability. From a social psychological perspective the precise medical category of disability is not particularly relevant — except if it carries a social stigma. *Severity* of disability is a more useful approach since this indicate the likely degree to which the disabled person will be able to cope with the problems of everyday living; this approach pervades the literature on rehabilitation. But we want to consider disabled men and women in their social context, and so we may tentatively divide this hetero-geneous group into five psycho-social categories of disability-handicap.

(1) This category is based on the degree to which the disability prevades the perceptual field. It is *highly visible* and provides early information which acts as an anticipatory signal to others (the blind person's white cane, the paraplegic's wheelchair). These signals convey clues about the social identity of the disabled person.

(2) In this category the dominant theme is difficulty in effective *interpersonal communication*. Distant cues may be absent or minimal but problems of reception or expression occur early in

any social encounter; deafness and speech impediments are typical examples.

(3) Here the person appears normal both from a distance and during social encounters. His disability is *episodic* or *phasic* as with asthma, epilepsy, haemophilia and maladjustment.

(4) This category relates to the connotation carried by the label: the disability is associated with *social stigma*, as in severe retardation and educational subnormality.

(5) A *combination* of the above — for example Down's Syndrome (mongolism) with its physical aspect and its social stigma (1 and 4).

These categories can be used as discrete entities but also as dimensions, so that category (1), visible handicaps, may be considered as a range or continuum from highly visible to almost undetectable, and (2) as a range of communication defects from slight to severe; (3) is more useful as an inclusive group but (4) can be used discriminatively according to the degree of stigma attached. If recent research into childhood handicaps is a guide, then most of disabled persons cannot be adequately embraced by just one of these categories.

The categories are derived from observations of disabled persons' reception in our society and of our attitudes towards them. We know from the work of Cook (1971) and Argyle (1975) that the process of forming impressions of others is a complicated affair involving *static* elements — the face in repose, physique, voice, clothes, hairstyle, cosmetics, etc. — and *dynamic* aspects such as orientation, distance, posture, gesture, body movement, facial expression, gaze direction, tone of voice, rate and fluency of speech. Physique and appearance are important criteria in impressionistic social classification. The unusually tall woman, the obese child, the finely proportioned dancer or athlete call attention to themselves. Adams and Cohen (1974) have shown that teachers are influenced by their pupils' appearance, though only for a short while, after which other characteristics (learning and behaviour) become more significant. Nevertheless, physique and appearance are not unimportant in the forming of initial impressions. We can effect certain modifications to the flow of personal information given by our appearance but these are clearly limited. Moreover we learn, and so must the visibly handicapped, the specific cultural values (both positive and negative) attached to variations in physique and appearance. These values are of course, not simply applied to others, they are applied by the self to the self. Their acquisition is a long process begun in childhood, continued through a host of social encounters and powerfully reinforced by the media's projection of what is beautiful and desirable — and what is not. It is more than the ranking of self and others in some pecking order of good looks. A positively or a negatively valued physique and appearance can mean the attribution of other personal qualities and characteristics which follow the value direction of the physical variation. The exterior man reflects the inner one; folk-sayings, Latin tags, poetry and novels are rich with examples of perceived links between appearance and personality.

How we come to attach visual, social and moral meanings to physical variations is a process not clearly understood, but chance meetings with the disabled vividly illustrate for each of us the lesson we unconsciously learned in childhood. In encounters with the visibly disabled, the disability or disfigurement seems to dominate the perceptual field of both participants, so that what is central is the disability and not the disabled person. Physical variations signalled from afar, do of course, allow the non-handicapped to avoid a potential encounter or to prepare for it. The physical cues given by someone who violates physical conventions may make another person uncertain and awkward since a range of customary interpersonal skills — dynamic as well as static — will be seen to need modification or different emphasis. An additional hindrance to smooth interaction will be the experience of the one and the inexperience of the other. The normal person's limited contact with the handicapped people may make him uncertain and insecure in handling his side of an encounter, while the disabled person, from many previous experiences, may expect the encounter to be strained.

It has been suggested that in initial encounters the disabled person is never sure which aspect of him will be used — will the other concentrate on his disability (by asking indiscreet questions) or will he avoid it at all costs and never let it intrude even by so much as an incautious glance? Again there is more at work than mechanisms of interaction since also involved is the psychological meaning given to the disability by the other person.

Disability can mean different things to different people. In some it evokes a sympathetic response, in others a negative hostile reaction, and others again may wish simply to avoid the issue. Consequently, in terms of social psychology, initial encounters between the disabled and others do not start from a neutral point, and the disabled person has to deal with definitions of himself and his disability previously and independently conceived by others.

Where the disability is effectively non-visible to casual inspection but becomes apparent with any attempt at conversation, one participant would have been expecting a conventional encounter. It may be that unexpected communication difficulties have a greater impact than when anticipatory social defences are alerted. As the Royal National Institute for the Deaf advertise, 'It's a pity deaf people look so normal'. Mrs Abrahams, a university graduate with a hearing handicap, has written an account of some of her experiences in local politics ('reduced to the role of non-speaking server of coffee and biscuits'), with her children's friends, and visiting schools. 'I dread even going ... because it is always possible that some mother taken in by my normal appearance will try to open a conversation with me, will be answered by something unintelligible ... will be disconcerted and embarrassed, and I shall feel myself a blot on the landscape, a disgrace to the children' (Abrahams, 1973). Here the anticipatory mechanisms at work in the handicapped person encourage the avoidance of contact with others. For the non-handicapped the social and personal cost of meeting persons with communication difficulties makes for brief rather than sustained encounters. Once an encounter has begun there is no way of avoiding the centrality of the handicap, since an encounter is a process of communication and the handicap works against it. Communication, especially speech, is one of the hallmarks of membership of the human club, and those who cannot receive or express the spoken word are sometimes denied full rights within it.

Our third category is where there are no overt signs of handicap nor are there problems of communication; persons in this category 'pass' as conventional but their social orthodoxy is threatened by the episodic nature of their handicap. Persons with epilepsy or asthma are examples; when not having an asthmatic attack or an epileptic seizure, they can sustain a normal role. Although these conditions are very different from each other in origins and symptoms, psychologically they are similar since their manifestation is irregular and unpredictable. This means a background of psychological stress, and for persons so handicapped the constant theme of social experience is the threat of self-violation of normal identity — the possibility of discovery.

Some handicapping conditions impose on the sufferer a marked degree of negative attitudes. Severe mental retardation is an example of a condition associated with profound stigma. It may or may not be linked with visible signs, but is not infrequently connected with inappropriate or unusual social behaviour. Interaction between normal and retarded people is characteristically at an infantile level, but in general, encounters tend to be confined to those with a professional concern for the stigmatized person and his or her immediate family. The adult-child quality of relationships was noted by Kathleen Jones (1975, pp.108-10) in her observation of the behaviour of nurses in a hospital for the mentally handicapped. Nurses, she writes,

> ... see themselves as parents and their patients as children. The model of family behaviour is a legitimate one in helping dependent people but there are consequential problems such as the spread of authority to all aspects of the patient's life; the application of punishment to patients that nurses would apply to their own children and expectations that patients should respond to care with ... affection, obedience and gratitude.

Our final category is that reserved for the most afflicted — those who combine visible signs of their infirmity with difficulties in communication and who are also sometimes stigmatized. Here we may presume that conventional social behaviour suffers the greatest constraints.

The above categories illustrate, in a primitive way, some of the psycho-social dimensions of the problem of the disabled person as a social being. Disability is not only a medical matter, it is an area of concern for the social psychologist. According to Meyerson (1955, p.12) it is not an 'objective thing in a person but a social value judgement'. Perhaps it would be more correct to say that a disability may be evaluated objectively, in the sense that constraints on mobility, manipulatory skills, hearing, etc., can be quantified, but that the handicapping nature of the disability cannot be so accurately assessed. This will depend on the individual person's perception of his difficulties and whether the social climate either encourages or inhibits his striving to compensate for them. It is both a social value judgement and a personal one — a self-value judgement which is, of course, powerfully affected by the attitudes of, and interaction with others, but is not totally conditioned by them. Any loss of physical function is likely to be viewed negatively, and the negative values derive from three sources: the nature of the disability, negative values imposed by the self, and negative ones imposed by society.

Those who wish to emphasize the effect of social attitudes on the adjustment of disabled persons tend to neglect or underestimate the fact that physical disability does put problems in the way of attaining ordinary life goals. The practical difficulties of getting around in a wheelchair, or being a blind parent coping with an active toddler, are real enough. There are daily reminders of obstacles to achieving those things which the non-disabled take for granted, and failure in them is often the sharpest reminder of disability.

Continued failure may mean that some disabled people reduce their expectations, and in extreme cases may so restrict themselves as to be unable to sustain a viable self-image. Cumulative failure means frustration and personal devaluation, though the limitation which the disability imposes may be less than that which the person imposes on himself. If continued over a long period, the restriction on activities and experiences will eventually restrict the kind of person he is. Such negative self-evaluation may have its roots in the temperament or personality of the disabled person, or in his acceptance and application to himself of others' evaluation of his disability. Rehabilitation workers have observed this in the adventitiously handicapped who, after their injury, apply to themselves those attitudes about physical variations which formerly they shared with others.

Other people's attitudes to disability are the social and psychological 'matrix' in which the disabled person lives. It is fundamental to his socialization and is influential both in interpersonal behaviour and in the more organized ways in which society provides for the disabled. It includes the everyday sanction imposed by normals; differing socio-personal distances in interactions, and the laws, acts and institutions through which public attitudes are conveyed. The attitude of the dominant majority, expressed in informal interaction, legislation, social policy, and professional care agencies, creates a climate in which the disabled see how they are seen.

Attitudes to disability

It has been suggested that the behaviour, self-image and socialization of the disabled are conditioned by society's attitudes and the values that underpin them. Later we shall treat this topic more systematically, but for the present it is sufficient to ask some questions. Attitudes to handicap are not uniform but are subject to transformation and even radical change, and they vary according to the nature of the disability. The questions are: what is the range of attitudes present in our society, and is their variation systematically related to factors such as sex, social class or race? Is there a relationship between information, contact and attitudes to handicap? What is the relationship between expressed public sentiments and private behaviour? When attitudes change, what is the most effective vehicle of change — the media, pressure groups or the economic climate?

Some writers (Berreman, 1954; Tenny, 1953) have suggested that the prevailing social attitudes to disablement have led to the creation for the disabled of a social status somewhat like that given to ethnic minority groups. Both have a status subordinate to majority interests and suffer restrictions on entry into certain roles. Both appear to experience difficulties in employment and education. However, the disabled person is not usually a member of a group. He is often isolated and must meet the privations of his low status without the morale of group membership. While belonging to an ethnic minority group allows a person to attribute his low status to the oppressive attitude of the dominant majority, the disabled are more likely to put their equivalent status down to personal inadequacy.

Perhaps it would be more accurate to liken the social status of the disabled to that of adolescents making the transition from childhood to adulthood. Adolescents' status is marginal between the two — and the disabled are similarly marginal people. They occupy a position along the continuum from physically capable to physically helpless. The sense of marginality is intensified by the indefinite boundary between physical normality and physical disability. The characteristic psychological state that results is anxiety and insecurity. For the adolescent the pressing question is: 'Shall I be expected to behave as an adult or a child?' For the disabled the equivalent question is: 'Which part of myself is to be emphasized — the disabled or non-disabled aspect?' There is of course, a difference between the marginality of the adolescent and that of the disabled. That of the adolescent is temporary; that of the disabled may well be life-long.

Society is positive towards contributions from its members that stabilize and maintain social cohesion. Among these are productive capacity, responsible citizenship and conventional role-taking in major socialization agencies, e.g. the family. According to Levine (1970), the visibly disabled seem to communicate significant information about their potential contribution which they consider is often underestimated. Partly, this derives from stereotyped views of them and of their capacity for conventional social roles, and of course, the views are not wholly shared by the disabled themselves. Levine (p.43) is inclined to the opinion that society perceives the disabled in terms of categories and attributes:

> Society 'understands' or conceptualizes the disabled in categorical terms. Those attributes which society utilizes for categorizing the disabled we term the defining attributes of the category. Each behaviour in the category has a degree of defining value in respect of its predictability to the stereotype. Those behaviours which afford maximum prediction to the category have a high defining value and are crucial to the stability of the category. Although categories may be modified in relation to a particular individual to a great degree they represent categorizations based on biological resemblances.

Those aspects of the disabled person, and especially those physical ones which society regards as differentiating him most from others, are the *defining attributes*. But the disabled person also has his own perception of which aspects of his body, skills and limitations actually distinguish him from the non-handicapped. Those which he regards as critical in separating him off are the *criterial attributes*, and there can be discrepancies between defining and criterial attributes. When these discrepancies are large, personal insecurity is potentially maximized as the individual perception of self conflicts with stereotyped expectations. The process of 'getting the handicapped to accept their handicap' is one which attempts to narrow the gap between defining and criterial attributes. That the disabled are antagonistic to the way society defines them is shown by the presence within the traditional voluntary organizations of radical groups who are attempting to obtain some self-determination in the management of their affairs.

Levine suggests that attitudes to the handicapped are not static but evolve through at least five stages.

(1) All persons with a particular disability are held to possess certain characteristics.
(2) While general beliefs are held about a category of disability, an individual is seen as transcending the popular view: he is untypical of his category and this is explained by special circumstances such as intense motivation or exceptional compensating gifts.
(3) With sufficient examples of exceptional behaviour that portion of the defining attribute is dropped from the stereotype.
(4) Through medical and technical skills the disabled person is largely indistinguishable from the rest of his social group ('you'd never guess he was handicapped').
(5) By their skills, achievements and diversity of social roles, the collection of defining attributes vanishes, the true extent of individual differences is revealed and stereotyping does not take place.

Whether the process is as Levine described is open to investigation. The notion that we use convenient conceptual packages when thinking about others is, of course, not new. Perceptions of national characteristics, racial groups and other 'outsider' minorities are part of our social education: they are built-in elements in our socialization. To be 'like us' is natural and normal, to be 'not like us' is foreign, unusual and abnormal. Physical disability is perceived as a violation of physical normality that easily extends to social abnormality.

Normality and abnormality

The word 'normal' has several usages. Murphy (1972) deals with seven: most representative of its class, commonly encountered in its class, most suitable to survive, carrying no penalty, commonly aspired to, most perfect of its class and a statistical distribution with known characteristics. 'Normal' is a classificatory term and as such is useful when to group objects and events under a common heading increases our understanding. When the classification involves people and carries penalties or rewards it is vital that the process is clearly understood, open and rational. One of the more critical areas is that involving judgements about normal and abnormal behaviour, and then the border zone between the two is particularly important. Murphy (1973), examining the classifying of people as normal or abnormal in intelligence or social competence, thinks that the demarcation line is not precise. The process, he feels, is both arbitrary and expedient, and is compounded by significant errors in measurement or evaluation and by the intrusion of subjective judgement. Furthermore the line between normal and abnormal is so adjusted as to produce a deviant population of 'just manageable proportions'. Does a similar process operate in attitudes towards the disabled — is society readjusting its views of the extent of deviance it can tolerate?

Mercer (1972), in her examination of mild mental retardation, argues that the distinction between this and normality is related to two perspectives — a clinical and social-system one. The clinical perspective is divided into two models — medical and psychological. The medical model treats retardation as a defect in the individual, and his symptoms as the signs of an underlying cause of the retardation. This view locates the condition *within* the person and tends to discount socio-cultural factors except when they are directly implicated in the pathology. This makes 'normal' a residual category. The psychological model defines retardation in statistical terms: IQ below a standard deviation from the mean indicates a departure from the statistical norm. However, IQ is a value-laden characteristic in our society, low IQ scores are not simply statistical statements but become moral judgements. Like Murphy, Mercer is also concerned at the technical inadequacies of the means of measurement and also their misuse, e.g. when tests standardized on majority cultures are used to penalize minorities.

The clinical perspective contrasts with the social-system perspective, which recognizes that within each social system there are certain role expectations which vary with status and position, and that these expectations become the core of the normative structure. Behaviour which fulfils expectations will be seen as 'normal'. The retarded person is one whose behaviour is seen to violate or fail to meet expectations associated with roles. When judgements are made on socio-behavioural grounds, then the social context in which they are formed becomes critical in understanding how people are categorized. Filstead (1972) has shown that distinctions between conventional and unconventional behaviour are often ambiguous. Mercer argues, powerfully, that in the designation of normal and abnormal some individuals and social groups are more vulnerable than others. This suggests that an analysis of visible disability similar to Levine's could well be applied to those handicapping conditions associated with stigma.

Neither the minutiae of interactional behaviour nor the division of abnormals from normals provide a sufficiently dynamic framework for considering the handicapped person in society. That provided by 'misfit sociology' appears to do so.

Misfit sociology encapsulates a view of society developed in the 1960s which incorporates a variety of theoretical prespectives on deviants and deviancy. It includes crime, delinquency, counter-cultures, mental illness and disability. The older view of society's misfits had an image of deviance as 'something pathological or under-socialized', which in turn *explained* the deviant and his behaviour (Pearson, 1975). Society's role in the creation of deviance and the complex web of interaction that this implied was underplayed. The newer view favours taking into account the opinions and values of the deviant through direct observation, participant observation (becoming a member of a group under study and sharing their experiences) and the use of source material supplied by the deviants themselves. At the heart of this view is the belief that deviancy is not simply the property or pathology of an individual but a socially constructed state which emerges from an interaction between the deviant and the social order in which he lives. Perceptions of 'differences' between ourselves and others affect our responses to them and the expectations we have of them.

Our responses to deviancy at the level of casual encounters, or in professional-care relationships, the type and nature of institutional provision and the legislative framework, all reflect the interactive relationships between the deviant and society.

Disability as deviance

We have accumulated sufficient empirical evidence (e.g. Wright, 1960; Scott, 1969) and evidence from autobiographies (Brown, 1954; Minton, 1974) to claim that the physically disabled are given a socially constructed deviant status which can be placed within the 'misfit' model. The major positions supporting the model are predominantly interaction theories which, crudely summarized, suggest three views of man and his social behaviour. Firstly, individual behaviour is a response to the behaviour of others — a reciprocal influencing of people and social forces. Secondly, this reciprocal process implies the use of symbols as mediators, the chief of them being language, so that the influence is seldom direct, but by and through language. Thirdly, the self is part of the interaction matrix and is affected by the activities and outcomes of the process.

Interactions are seen by some writers as episodes of exchange where psychological 'goods' are the commercial currency. In exchanges, norms of reciprocal behaviour are created out of mutual obligation (not necessarily involving calculation) and are part of the social bonding mechanisms by which social identities are constructed and maintained. Considering the disabled in interactional settings — what sort of goods do they bring to the transactions? Richardson (1968), writing on the socialization of the handicapped child, notes that in growing up the normal child forms more and more voluntary relationships which are increasingly outside family control; these depend for their continuity on an exchange of goods that is not one-sided. Some disabilities by their nature appear to reduce the potential for reciprocal behaviour — it may be inhibited by the failure of the handicapped to provide selectively the non-verbal companions of speech. Interactions are monitored by the 'unique sociological functions of the eye' (Goffman, 1969) and the blind are unable to use it. The significance of glance and gaze is widely accepted (Argyle, 1973), and failure to supply such accessories of conventional communication may prevent the disabled from being able to offer sufficient reinforcement for sustained inter-action. The deaf person's difficulties in communicating may suggest to others that the cost-benefit ratio is too unequal to make enduring relationships worthwhile. The deviance of handicapped persons arises from their apparently negligible potential for interaction.

Deviance not only stigmatizes the deviant, but those in regular association with him. This phenomenon is described by Goffman (1968, p.43) as a 'tendency for stigma to spread from the stigma-tized individual to his close connections', from which it follows that such 'courtesy stigma' is generally avoided rather than sought. The concept of stigma is closely allied to the process of labelling described by Pearson (1975).

Whether a physical or mental deviation is regarded as stigma-tizing depends on how people respond to the particular label — what Becker (1963) referred to as 'the consequences of the application by others of rules and sanctions to an offender'. We have already noted that Meyerson (1955) saw disability as a social value judgement — a negative one. For Goffman, stigma meant the imputation to a person of attributes that are deeply discrediting. Despite changes in attitudes, the disabled are still treated as having a stigma, although the more blatant forms of prejudice are camouflaged. When confronted by discrimination, hostility, indif-ference or simply awkwardness, the disabled person will naturally tend to withdraw from interpersonal or community transactions, thereby ' ... lessening the possibilities of understanding his inter-ests, aspirations and the ways of dealing with society's perception of his deviance' (Levine, 1970, p.45).

The distinction, developed by Lemert (1967), between primary and secondary deviances is of value here. The primary deviance is the disability itself, while the secondary deviance is an adaptive pattern of behaviour for coping with the social responses to the primary one. The work of Scott (1969, 1970) on the socialization of the blind illustrates this dual nature of disability as deviance. Visual handicap is the primary deviance, while the secondary one is the behaviour which develops as a result of blind people's day-to-day encounters with the sighted community, and the attitudes and expectations of professional agencies and 'blindness workers'. In Scott's opinion one of the chief aims of the latter is to socialize the blind into holding self-perceptions which correspond to those held about blindness by the workers themselves and their agencies. Minton's account (1974) of his experience as a middle-aged man who became blind is the story of his struggle to affirm his identity and individuality in the face of a powerful and compassionate official ideology of blindness, and of his rejection of the role of 'blind man' — preferring his own definition of self, which was unchanged except by the cruel addition of the primary deviance.

Interpersonal behaviour and labelling are linked by the view that concepts of self and social roles are both learned in personal relationships. It has been argued that the self is 'penetrated' by others whom we meet and by their response to us. For the disabled this penetration, the basic means by which the self is evaluated, is qualitatively different from the experience of the majority because of the practical difficulties in communication that arise from the primary deviance, and because of the secondary deviance that accompanies stigmatization and stereotyping. Davis (1964) places initial interaction between normals and the visibly disabled at the level of 'fictionalized acceptance', the quality of interacting being starved and kept at bare subsistence. If the content, style and frequency of encounters is impoverished, brief and occasional, then people at the receiving end of such experiences are likely to develop a distorted view of social roles and the self.

Roles are mechanisms by which a person participates in his social context, and some sociologists (e.g. Thomas, 1966) see constraints on the roles available to the disabled (limitations on conventional role-taking, accompanied by their expecting specific roles associated with being handicapped). Thomas distinguished five disability-related roles: the disabled patient; the handicapped performer; the helped person; the disability co-manager; and the public relations man for his type of disability. These roles are created for the disabled from perceptions and expectations, and express a deviant status. One effect of such role requirements is to entice the disabled into adopting coping strategies, such as maintaining a non-threatening social distance, forms of impression management which minimize the disability's obtrusiveness, and the concealment of information which might be discrediting. In total, this means the stage-managing of a phantom acceptance of the given deviant status.

Misfit sociology has been criticized for its theoretical vagueness and its reliance on inside accounts, while Goffman's stance has been challenged for its unattractive view of man — as always attempting to win support for the presented self. More serious, however, is the charge that it has failed to provide a commanding view of society and instead has concentrated on what its critics have termed the trivia of interpersonal behaviour. These criticisms are not without validity, but misfit sociology has among its positive contributions the power to illuminate our own part and that of professional caring persons in creating deviance, as well as providing a platform for views from the 'other side'. As regards disability it allows the use of diverse sources, personal accounts as well as traditional modes of investigation and a range of theoretical positions. All this is an advantage given the absence of a single comprehensive theory of the social psychology of disability.

The misfit model is thus admirably suited for explaining people accorded deviant status. But amongst the handicapped there are some who appear to avoid the stigma attached to others with the same affliction. Are these persons to be understood as having exceptional compensating endowments or unusual opportunities?

Pro-social behaviour

The misfit model is also inadequate for dealing with man as a social animal who responds positively to the needs of others. Altruism, pro-social behaviour, helping, volunteering, gift-sharing are the other side of the coin. All imply a degree of self-sacrificial behaviour, and so may be taken as some of man's more attractive features. Even this, however, has been opposed — by the view that they are responses of individuals with unrepresentatively low self-esteem who indulge in altruistic behaviour as an opportunity to assert a more favourable self-image. Krebs (1970), in a review of research and theories about pro-social behaviour, notes that it challenges global theories of man as self-seeking and egoistic. Krebs acknowledges that the definition of altruistic behaviour is uncertain and its motivation not well understood: it may be a response to a temporary psychological state following feelings of success or competence, or may spring from the beneficial effects of an example of altruism. But in some individuals it is more than a temporary state, being so firmly part of them that it deserves the status of a trait. Pro-social behaviour is certainly elicited by dependence on the part of the recipient, and appears to be affected by perceptions of whether the dependence is externally or internally caused and the attractiveness of the dependent person. It has been shown that females are more altruistic towards the more deeply dependent than are males; developmentally there is evidence of an increase in pro-social behaviour in children as they mature; and there are some studies showing social-class differences (for example, in Britain fostering is mainly undertaken by working-class families).

The history of medical, legal, educational and vocational safeguards and opportunities for the handicapped provides strong evidence of individuals capable of generosity and selfless behaviour, and similar people exist today. Benedict Nightingale (1973) has shown that charity is a complex affair, sometimes based on self-glorification but not inevitably so, as Titmuss (1970) in his work on blood donations illustrates. In that wonderfully rich book, Titmuss maintains that as society becomes more complicated and the care of the sick and needy more the responsibility of the state, giving becomes more, rather than less, important since it concentrates on ' ... processes, transactions and institutions which promote an individual's sense of identity, participation and community, and allows him more freedom of choice for the expression of altruism ...'. But perhaps the most distinctive note struck by Titmuss is to link the individual act of donation and the structural framework. Writing about the National Health Service, he notes that the 'most unsordid act of British social policy in the twentieth century has allowed and encouraged sentiments of altruism, reciprocity and social duty to express themselves ... ' (Titmuss, 1970, p.225). That is, altruism is removed from the unsupported individual act and the paternalism of the philanthropist, and becomes part of a wider pattern of social behaviour which encourages both.

2 Handicapped children

Classification

According to Fowler's *Dictionary of Modern English Usage* the '…use of handicapped as a euphemism descriptive of children not fully equipped mentally or physically is recent' (Fowler, 1975, p.238). The *Oxford English Dictionary* dates from 1823 the use of the word in the general sense of any 'encumbrance that weighs upon effort'. While there is a certain appeal about plain language that refers to the hearing-impaired as deaf and the physically handicapped as cripples, the term 'handicapped' in the general sense is surely preferable to those which have such obviously negative connotations. If to call 'handicapped' the group of children with encumbrances that weigh upon effort is euphemistic, so be it. They have enough burdens without the additional one of unflattering language.

Within the wide term 'handicapped children' several systems of subclassification are possible. On such system is based on medical judgement — for example, when physically handicapped children are classified by major family of disease or disability, such as cerebral palsy, spina bifida, or muscular dystrophy. Each of these has further subdivisions depending on specific forms, causes and prognosis: thus, doctors speak of athetoid (slow writhing movements) or ataxic (marked lack of the sense of balance) forms of cerebral palsy. Medical classification is often the main system but it is not the only one. Included amongst 'handicapped children' are also those whose 'encumbrance' is not physical or sensory, but behavioural. Those children who have limited mental abilities or disorders of emotion or social adjustment (the educationally subnormal, the maladjusted) are also embraced by the broad term. Clearly this type of classification relies on psychological and educational criteria.

The classification used by the Department of Education and Science in providing special educational treatment for handicapped children is another system, based on perceived educational needs, and it illustrates the diversity of conditions we are dealing with. The DES divides the children as follows: blind, partially sighted, deaf, partially hearing, physically handicapped, delicate, maladjusted, educationally subnormal, epileptic, speech defect and autistic. Of course any such system has its arbitrary elements. Research has shown that handicapped children do not fall neatly into these subdivisions; many have handicaps additional to their primary disability — indeed in some cases it is hard to determine what *is* the primary disability (Rutter, Tizard and Whitmore, 1970). There has been dissatisfaction with the present system (Younghusband, 1970) and fairly recently the DES has developed an assessment approach which seems to override the classification of children on medical grounds and concentrates on psychological or educational need (DES, 2/75).

Whether medical classification can be equated with educational need is a question we shall return to, but at least the former is relatively unambiguous. The same cannot be said for where psychological or educational criteria are concerned. Categorization of children as educationally subnormal or maladjusted is full of difficulties and uncertainties. Maladjustment, in particular, is a condition perhaps more easily recognized than defined, and there is little agreement about its meaning, symptoms or treatment (Bridgeland, 1971; Whitmore, 1975). Educational subnormality is equally open to objection. Both require selective social judgements. However, the wrangling over terms need not detain us — for our purposes we may take the situation as it exists. Children are identified (by various agencies) as having a disability — physical or psychological — and this is a signal for action, which may be the placement of children in special schools. The criteria that *should* apply to such placements are not our concern here, although the issue is of great importance. The placement of a child in a particular social context can be assumed to confer on that child a particular social identity. Thus, placement in a school for the blind confers on a child the identity of blindness whether or not that classification is suspect or accurate. And social identity *is* subject to transformation: a 'healthy' child may be deemed 'sick', and a 'sick' child 'healthy'. The identity given may or may not be permanent but its determination is largely outside the child's control. He is powerless against a system which classifies him and may reclassify him. Only when he becomes an adult does he have some hand in shaping his personal and social identity.

From the perspective of social psychology the distinctions noted in the first chapter between visible disabilities, episodic conditions, stigmatized ones and combinations of these are valid when considering the social behaviour of others towards handicapped children. However, to comprehend the complex processes which shape the developing child other factors will need to be considered. These include the social systems involved such as the family, school and peer groups, and the fact that the disabled child may easily be considered a member of a minority group.

Child health — a changing pattern

One of the most striking features of the history of childhood disability, particularly in the last century, is the change that has taken place in the nature and prevalence of handicapping conditions. A dramatic symbol of the improvement in the health and well-being of children is their greater life expectancy today than a hundred years ago — it is, in fact, thirty years greater (Henderson, 1974). To illustrate the gain made in this area, Henderson records that if the death rate from communicable diseases of children under 15 years of age had remained unchanged over the last century, there would now be 70,000 deaths per year instead of 400. In more recent times, polio affected 2,700 children in 1947, and 9 in 1971. In 1907 tuberculosis was a killer claiming some 3,000 child victims, a figure which declined to 4 in 1971. The changes are not only reflected in the improved survival rates, but recovery from many conditions can now be complete whereas formerly it was often only partial. The sulpha drugs and antibiotics have been critical in this area. Equally important has been the advance in surgical skills, while for the future such practices as amniocentesis (intra-uterine examination of the unborn child) and genetic counselling promise to reduce the incidence of seriously handicapping conditions. The 1970 programme of vaccinating teenage schoolgirls against German measles is a further example of how the pattern of handicapping conditions can be subject to rapid change. Clearly, however, the specific advances in medical, surgical and nursing skills have to be placed against the backcloth of the general increase in standards of health, diet and hygiene which has been such a factor in the health history of the last hundred years.

But the overall picture of improvements is not without its share of setbacks, and three examples can show how new problems can obtrude themselves.

(a) In 1948 there was a rapid increase in the number of babies with visual defects. This increase continued until around 1955, when it was found that blindness could occur in low-weight, premature babies who were given life-saving oxygen, which unfortunately damaged the tissue behind the lens of the eye, especially in the retina. Several hundred babies in this country were affected.

(b) Spina bifida is the abnormal development during the intra-uterine period of one or two vertebrae, causing the posterior part to remain divided; the cleft in the spine can be small (not resulting in any disability) or very large with massive disturbance to the muscles and nerves below the site of the cleft. In the most severe form of the condition (myelomeningocele) the spinal chord may be malformed allowing infection to enter the cleft. Through skillful surgery it became possible for many more children with the condition to survive. Indeed so successful was medical intervention in the 1960s that there was a consequential change in the child population in schools for the physically handicapped, and the spina bifida group became one of the largest categories. The number of spina bifida cases became a cause for concern and there was (and still is) a continuing debate within the medical profession and among the general public over the wisdom of keeping infants alive regardless of the severity of the disability. The medico-ethical problems posed by advances in surgical techniques are formidable; but there is some evidence, however, that the number of operations on children with this condition has declined since 1970 (Adelstein, 1976).

(c) The third example is the well-publicized case of the sudden increase in the number of children born with limbs deformed or absent in 1961-2. This was the thalidomide tragedy. It is a paradox that while medical skill has significantly reduced the incidence of certain handicapping conditions, the same skill has enabled more and more children with graver disabilities to survive.

The DES data in Table 2.1 show the number and categories of handicapped children attending special schools; the extent to which there are gross differences in the incidence of the various main categories of handicap; and where over the period 1950-74 there has been little change in provision (e.g. for blindness) or where the change has been great, e.g. the growth in provision for maladjusted children and those with speech problems. These figures do not provide a complete guide to the incidence of handicapping conditions in childhood since many disabled children are in ordinary schools. In 1968 there were 2,765 children with cerebral palsy attending special schools and a further 1,500 in ordinary ones. At the same time there were 500 children with muscular dystrophy in special schools and a further 500 in ordinary schools. This is part of the changing pattern of provision, with a slow but sure tendency on the part of more and more ordinary schools to admit disabled pupils (Anderson, 1973).

Attitudes to handicapped children

De Mause (1976) has written that the history of children is a nightmare from which we are only slowly awakening. Children are the missing group in the political and economic accounts of the past. Coveney records that the child did not exist as an important and continuous theme in English literature until the 1790s. For Coveney the emergence of the child as a literary symbol at the same time as there were significant social, economic and political changes

Table 2.1 Special schools, full-time pupils and teachers, 1950 to 1975 at January (DES, 1976)

	1950	1955	1960	1965	1970	1971	1972	1973	1974	1975
Hospital schools										
Schools										
Maintained	95	105	92	82	80	77	147	146	147	152
Non-maintained	15	15	13	10	9	9	8	9	8	7
Total	110	120	105	92	89	86	155	155	155	159
Full-time pupils										
Boys	3,604	3,477	2,692	2,271	2,012	2,033	5,106	5,689	5,523	5,635
Girls	2,972	2,999	2,159	1,694	1,493	1,504	3,520	3,986	3,930	4,037
Total	6,576	6,476	4,851	3,965	3,505	3,537	8,626	9,675	9,453	9,672
Teachers										
Full-time teachers	507	576	523	448	461	472	1,105	1,207	1,028	1,111
Full-time equivalent of part-time teachers	—	6	12	14	16	19	37	38	44	39
Other special schools										
Schools										
Maintained	393	514	598	678	788	828	1,242	1,277	1,315	1,337
Non-maintained	98	109	117	112	109	105	104	105	105	107
Day	299	321	382	454	536	562	949	977	1,019	1,019
Boarding	192	302	333	336	361	371	397	405	401	425
Total	491	623	715	790	897	933	1,346	1,382	1,420	1,444
Full-time pupils by category of major handicap										
Blind Boys	610	656	718	681	601	613	566	588	587	644
Girls	469	540	582	536	498	480	465	490	469	515
Partially-sighted Boys	853	1,081	1,103	1,115	1,248	1,265	1,319	1,302	1,304	1,331
Girls	705	761	689	734	712	731	747	782	803	896
Deaf Boys	1,844	2,218	1,932	1,721	1,841	1,900	1,893	1,927	1,985	2,098
Girls	1,408	1,697	1,531	1,389	1,522	1,571	1,559	1,593	1,627	1,705

Partially-hearing	Boys	566	700	812	933	1,120	1,140	1,178	1,249	1,285	1,340
	Girls	398	595	641	684	816	880	919	978	979	991
Physically handicapped	Boys	3,258	3,410	4,073	4,330	5,035	5,250	5,716	5,811	6,090	6,995
	Girls	3,138	2,903	2,976	3,155	3,795	3,882	4,115	4,224	4,399	5,229
Delicate	Boys	5,706	6,678	5,948	4,864	3,908	3,661	3,403	3,312	3,121	2,904
	Girls	5,047	5,589	4,672	3,602	2,542	2,315	2,151	2,008	1,891	1,817
Maladjusted	Boys	467	1,029	1,426	2,305	4,793	5,952	6,966	8,172	8,857	10,140
	Girls	120	206	316	599	1,300	1,814	1,986	2,322	2,726	3,387
Educationally subnormal	Medium Boys	9,205	13,633	19,640	25,571	31,388	31,996	45,894	46,946	32,069	31,727
	Severe Boys	–	–	–	–	–				15,480	11,290
	Medium Girls	5,968	9,011	13,175	17,099	20,380	20,847	31,707	32,610	21,284	21,017
	Severe Girls	–	–	–	–	–				11,371	8,602
Epileptic	Boys	433	475	416	464	581	632	744	811	860	1,294
	Girls	312	320	327	350	434	481	515	566	646	911
Speech defect	Boys	21	40	83	143	564	912	1,215	1,643	2,081	4,364
	Girls	15	16	39	59	264	502	599	795	1,034	2,529
Autistic	Boys	–	–	–	–	–	–	–	–	200	377
	Girls	–	–	–	–	–	–	–	–	76	165
Total	Boys	22,963	29,920	36,151	42,127	51,079	53,321	68,894	71,761	73,919	74,504
	Girls	17,580	21,638	24,948	28,207	32,263	33,503	44,763	46,368	47,305	47,764
	Total	40,543	51,558	61,099	70,334	83,342	86,824	113,657	118,129	121,224	122,268
Teachers	Full-time teachers	2,759	3,805	4,866	5,823	7,534	7,996	11,315	12,116	12,065	12,867
	Full-time equivalent of part-time teachers	–	108	154	265	412	395	473	515	484	522

Source: reproduced with the permission of the Controller of Her Majesty's Stationery Office.

(industrialization, urban growth and their accompanying psychological consequence — alienation) was no coincidence. The child
could serve as a symbol of the artist's dissatisfaction with society,
which was in process of such harsh development about him
(Coveney, 1967, p.31). Neither is it a coincidence that during this
period of the discovery of childhood as a legitimate literary image
the first efforts should also be made to provide sanctuary and
asylum for the most unfortunate children.

We cannot, perhaps, recapture the precise attitudes behind the
actions of the first people who gave concrete expression to their
desire to assist the handicapped. But from the kinds of institution
set up and their educational and religious regimes, we can glean
something of their attitudes and of those of their contemporaries.
Provision for handicapped children has three main themes — the
inspiration of individuals, the work of charitable bodies and,
progressively, the involvement of government. This pattern remains
the same today. Pioneer work by gifted teachers and the contribution
of voluntary societies still exist alongside state provision, and the
former are very often attracted to fields not yet receiving government
support. There is a continuous tradition from the end of the
eighteenth century to the present day of the combination of these
three elements (Pritchard, 1963). As historian of the process,
Pritchard has commented that the earliest schools for the handicapped had one major element in common — they were all residential.
This reflects the aspiration of their founders to provide a secure
asylum for the deaf, the dumb and the crippled. The schools had
something else in common — they were protective, steeped in
enthusiasm for religious observance, and their training programmes
were vocational rather than educational.

Not until after the 1870 Education Act did the state begin to be
formally responsible for provision for the handicapped. Acts of
1893 and 1899 enabled blind, deaf, epileptic and defective children to receive education, but this also followed the pattern of earlier
voluntary provision in being segregated, though not exclusively
residential. The Act of 1921 combined earlier legislation and
required that children be certified as mentally or physically defective before being placed in special schools, a device which undoub-
tedly contributed to the stigma which attached itself to these
schools. Following the Butler Act of 1944, the categories of

handicap were extended and the stage set for the expansion of special school places shown in Table 2.1, although the Act was clear that special schooling was only one form of special educational treatment. One of the most notable features of the Act, and subsequent regulations, was the defining of the categories of children requiring special help and the placing of a definite duty on Local Education Authorities to discover children with disabilities of body or mind and to determine and provide such special help as they required. That they have responded to this need is partly shown by the growth of special schools (from 491 in 1950 to 1444 in 1975).

Parallel and complementary to this has been the development of special classes and facilities in ordinary schools. The 1944 Act and subsequent regulations still regarded one group of children with severe cognitive and social limitations as ineducable, though they did consider them 'trainable'. Not until 1970 were mentally handicapped children formally admitted into the care of LEAs — for the first time all children were seen to be capable of benefiting from education; and the stigmatizing and incorrect label of 'ineducable' was finally discarded. While the main burden of provision falls on the LEAs, schools supported by independent and voluntary bodies continue their important work. Some independent schools are run by governing bodies which continue the work of the original founder. Their contribution is such that without them 'some severely handicapped cerebral palsied, autistic and epileptic children would be without education even today' (Pritchard, 1973, p.184).

This history of provision for handicapped children has been one of growth within the framework of a partnership between state and voluntary societies. There are still gaps and unevenness in the distribution of resources, but until fairly recently there was implicit acceptance of the nineteenth-century philosophy of segregation. That notion has now been seriously challenged and there is a strong movement seeking to re-examine it (Snowdon Working Party, 1976). There are those who argue that nothing except financial expediency stands in the way of having every handicapped child, no matter how serious his disability, placed in an ordinary school. This extreme view suggests that while there may be a need for separate special schools, many more children than once thought possible can with advantage go to ordinary schools. There has been a remarkable revolution in attitudes within (historically considered) a relatively short time and we have come from neglect and indifference, through protectiveness, to an acceptance not only that the disabled child has the right to the best medical treatment and care, but also that his disability ought not to be used as a device for separating him from society. While the changes are significant in terms of our own history, when we compare the rate of change here with events in other countries (most notably in Sweden) we may wonder why such developments have taken so long. Nevertheless, although the reasons for this change still need to be researched, what it represents is unambiguous.

The sociology of handicapped children

In 1954 Mendelsohn wrote about the contribution sociology could make to the study of mentally handicapped children. He suggested that the phenomenon of mental deficiency had certain social characteristics needing examination. The condition was not something which affected the child alone, but his brothers and sisters, his family, their relationships with relatives and neighbours, the local community, and ultimately the whole of society. He presented a simple model with three areas of particular interest — information and attitudes; parental reactions; and community programmes. The subject of mental deficiency, he wrote, is shrouded in 'myths, irrational taboos, negative stereotypes and misinformation' (Mendelsohn, 1954, p.506). Children labelled as deficient grow up in climates of belief and attitudes which affect the responses of others to them. The exploration of these attitudes is a prerequisite to understanding not only personal behaviour, but also the growth of institutional provision and the possible direction of social policy. Closely related to the range of attitudes in a community is the accuracy or otherwise of the information about the condition.

Mendelsohn's second area to be considered when examining the social experience of the handicapped child was that of parental reactions. He noted that the evidence at that time (confirmed by many subsequent investigations) was that parents' attitudes to a handicapped child were highly varied, ranging from acceptance, through indifference, to rejection. He saw this as a vital 'micro-attitude' climate which could be systematically investigated

— especially the possible relationships between attitudes and social class, attitudes and community response, attitudes and home or institutional care.

His third area, community programmes, focuses on the part played by organizations in securing better conditions for handicapped children. He thought it would be worthwhile to inquire what kinds of people are active in these organizations, what are their methods, how they transform themselves from local societies to national ones of considerable influence and prestige, how power passes from the dedicated volunteer to the professional organizer, and most crucial, how far organizations represent the views of those they purport to champion.

This basic approach was taken a stage further by Kurtz in 1964, in a discussion of the role of sociology in the study of mental retardation. He suggested that sociologists might concentrate upon three major themes: (a) extent, type and distribution; (b) social systems; and (c) attitudes. Though Kurtz was specifically concerned with retardation, they can be applied to any handicapping condition.

Discovering how a handicap is distributed, both geographically and socially, will lead to such questions as: is the condition overrepresented in one social group compared with another, and if so, why? Chief among the various social systems in contact with handicapped children are their immediate families, neighbours and the various institutions set up to deal with this type of disability.

Kurtz provides an example of how surveys of the distribution of retarded children and their families can produce some unexpected findings. In New York a study was carried out which asked the question: Of those children with IQs of under 50, which ones are placed in institutions? One finding was that placement was linked to the ethnic or religious background of the child's family. The committal rate for retarded Jewish children was 1:20; for white Protestants and Catholics, 1:10; for Negroes, 1:4; and Puerto Rican children 1:2. This suggests an interplay of economic, social and religious factors. The other major factor was the behaviour of the child, though not the behaviour *per se* but the social setting in which it took place. Unacceptable behaviour can be managed at home, but in public it has a different social meaning since it reveals the disparity between the child's age and his social development, and negative community reactions to this threaten the family's own self-definition of competence and control.

The study of social systems means that of roles. Kurtz calls for the study of the roles of those whose circumstances or professions bring them into contact with the retarded, and provides this provocative description of the role of the doctor:

> ... the primary responsibility of the physician in our society is to bring about complete, early and painless recovery of the patient. In this situation the doctor-patient relationship is an action-oriented situation. But what happens when the physician is in a situation in which he feels that his medical actions can accomplish little for the patient? Such a situation is, to say the least, extremely frustrating ....
>
> Many mentally retarded individuals present such a frustrating situation, since means have not been found to improve their mental condition by medical measures. Faced with this frustrating situation, what does the physician do, i.e. how does he purge himself of his feelings of inadequacy? Physicians in private practice can follow a definite routine — they can refer the patient to specialists who, if also private practitioners, can eventually refer the patient to an institution. But this procedure only shifts the problem through a series of medical practitioners until there can be no more shifting or reassignment of the case. The physician in the institution must, finally, face the problem. How does the physician in this 'final depository' clear the air for the entire medical profession and for himself? First, this is accomplished by carrying on a program of research aimed at paving the way for future medical treatment of the condition. Furthermore, the physician's action-orientation leads him to the medical treatment of other problems of the patient, although they may not be specifically related to his mental condition. Meanwhile there are efforts to educate and train the individual to his highest levels, hoping that he can find a place somewhere in society. (Kurtz, 1964, pp.18-19)

Like Mendelsohn, Kurtz lays great stress on the importance of public and professional attitudes about mental retardation, and particularly refers to the popular stereotypes of the personality of the retarded and to how attitudes may influence their social status.

The framework provided by Mendelsohn and Kurtz seems appropriate for the initial study of the broad social factors affecting any group of handicapped children. If they are combined, then the examination will embrace: (a) the extent and distribution of the condition; (b) public and professional attitudes (including the accuracy or otherwise of information); (c) social systems in contact with the children — especially the family and specialized institutions; the roles of members of the social systems.

There will, of course, be modifications and differences of emphasis depending on the particular nature of the handicaps being considered. Darbyshire (1970), in a plea for the systematic sociological study of deafness in children, argues that there are strong links between existing sociological studies and the world of deafness, particularly in three areas.

The deaf are a distinctive subculture similar to an ethnic minority culture. They are a disadvantaged group facing negative attitudes and discrimination in education and employment. Darbyshire draws a parallel between the segregated schooling of the black child and that of the deaf child: both encounter similar problems when attempts are made to integrate them into ordinary schools — transport difficulties, acceptance by peer groups, the convincing of parents and teachers that integrated schooling is desirable.

For Darbyshire deafness is a particular and severe form of *deprivation*. He suggests that in extreme cases the deaf child shows many of the characteristics of the culturally deprived child. The disadvantages of the deprived child have been laid at his parents' door — so also with deaf children whose academic success is vitally affected by the quality of home life.

Like the previous writers, Darbyshire, too, acknowledges the importance of family dynamics in understanding the deaf child. He details some of the aspects involved:

> Tests and scales exist for measuring social adjustment and other parameters of development and the factors to be assessed can probably be divided into what might be termed 'concrete' and 'abstract' influences. Among the concrete factors one would wish to examine are family size, family income and occupation, housing conditions, the number of toys and books at home,

whether or not both parents are working and the educational level of the parents. The abstract influences would include the attitude of the parents, siblings and neighbours to the child and his handicap and his attitude to them, the amount of time the parents spend 'working' with the child and the quality of the 'work' they do, the frequency and value of their contacts with the school and the effectiveness of the school's contact with them, the parents' aspirations for the child, the quality of language used in the home among parents and other siblings, the relationship between the parents and the impact which the birth of a deaf child has had on their marriage. (Darbyshire, 1970, p.4)

Obviously, Darbyshire's approach to the sociology of deafness has several similarities to Kurtz's proposals for the study of retardation.

Social experiences and personal development

The broad social factors dealt with above form, as it were, a backcloth against which the handicapped child grows and develops. Social psychology has as one of its concerns the influence of experience upon personal development — how the growing child behaves and reacts to the various social systems in which he participates. How, for instance, does he react to his disability, and is this reaction governed by the attitudes of those around him? Is maladjustment an inevitable consequence of disability or is it a handicap resulting from negative social encounters?

Hollinshead (1959) offers an appropriate caution here. Interest in the social and psychological adjustment mechanism of the disabled has led researchers to underestimate the true significance of the real limitations imposed by disability. He draws on studies comparing the development of children with cerebral palsy, blindness and deafness with that of normal children and concludes that most of the gross differences in ability, attainment and adjustment could be ascribed to the nature of the children's defects and were not secondary handicaps related to maladjustment. Here is a major challenge to research — to disentangle the real 'encumbrance' imposed by the disability from the handicaps which develop as the result of social experiences.

Trippe (1959), while acknowledging the real limitations of

disability, concludes that cumulative evidence of the degree of emotional disturbance and maladjustment in handicapped children needs to be explained and suggests that the Merton (1957) theory of social structure provides a guide. In particular, he uses Merton's concept that deviance, or pressure towards deviance, arises from the relationship between culturally defined goals and the approved means of reaching them. If society explicitly or implicitly suggests that the goals of life are success, status and prestige, then the pressure towards deviance increases if the approved means of attaining them are unequally distributed. When a person accepts the goals but these means are not available, he may resort to illegitimate ones. At all events, the drive for success when there is limited opportunity does create anxiety and, in extreme cases, personality disorganization.

Faced with incompatibility between goals and opportunities, a person may adopt a number of stances, e.g. a gradual reduction of the desired goals, which is possible when there are strong pressures to comply with generally approved methods of achievement and few avenues to success. Or it can lead to the abandonment of both the goals and the approved means. In some respects the handicapped child is insulated from many of these pressures though he will certainly experience them at adolescence. Trippe was convinced that evidence of rigidity, constricted personality and compulsiveness noted in some handicapped children, was consistent with their abandoning the goals of social success while retaining a belief in the conventional means of achieving them. Further evidence shows the progressive involvement of the handicapped with others like themselves and indicates an abandonment of community membership.

> It should be clear that lofty aspirations and limited realistic opportunities are precisely the condition which invite socially deviant behaviours. For people with limited opportunities, continued effort toward accepted goals using only the approved methods, while socially appropriate, may lead to personality disorganization. The poor reality testing and highly unrealistic goals observed in many atypical children illustrates this.
>
> (Trippe, 1959, p.173)

But how reliable is the evidence on 'poor reality testing', unrealistic goals, compulsive behaviour, rigidity and restricted personality in handicapped children? Reynolds (1960) challenges many of the assumptions that have been made about their personality and adjustment. He criticizes much of the evidence because it applies to *individuals* what has been discovered in *groups*. He uses the concept of 'the application to individuals of base-rate characteristics'; in many studies there has been over-emphasis on central tendencies and insufficient attention to variance. 'The deaf are properly resentful if they are thought of all as a class, or being non-verbal. The orthopaedically handicapped should not all be viewed as "isolates" or "rejectees" simply because a few studies have shown this central tendency for those of their physical status' (Reynolds, 1960, p.244). To concentrate the reporting of research findings on base-rate characteristics is to produce a misleading picture. Reynolds points out that the most forceful action is undertaken on behalf of the most grossly handicapped in a category, and this gives rise to an image which is then applied to others in the category even if they are only mildly handicapped. He is anxious to respect the variability of personality and adjustment within any group of handicapped children. Those readers with experience of such a group will sympathize, since what is prominent there *is* the variety of the children's behaviour, attainments, adjustment and personality. Base-rate characteristics may exist but they must only be applied to individuals with the utmost circumspection, as unfortunately they can be blown up into expectations.

An important element in the social psychology of handicapped children (and adults), touched on in chapter 1, is the nature and quality of interpersonal experiences. The existing climate of attitudes is the psychological setting in which so-called normals and handicapped persons come into contact. One of the ways of estimating initial willingness or otherwise to interact with the disabled is to measure perceived social distance, i.e. the degree to which people feel confortable or uncomfortable when meeting deviants in a variety of social settings. For example, a respondent may say that he would not object to working alongside a disabled workmate — but would not welcome him as a friend at a social gathering.

The establishment of social distance varies according to the type and severity of disability (e.g. blindness is usually less socially threatening than deafness), the experience and information the normal person has concerning the disability and according to certain personality traits. It is a reciprocal process since the disabled, as a result of their experiences, set up their own system of social distance. Previous negative social experiences may lead them to anticipate coolness or awkwardness, and this may increase the difficulties of interpersonal communication, reinforcing a belief that others hold negative attitudes towards them. Negative social reinforcement may encourage a disabled person to limit social interaction, thus confirming for others that he is 'difficult to get along with', and the combined effect is to prevent perceptions from becoming less stereotyped. Social distance mechanisms act in an anticipatory way — allowing both parties to avoid or to limit inter-action. For some disabled people loneliness is preferable to rebuff. For normal persons avoidance may be preferable to awkwardness.

Social interaction between handicapped persons and others has been studied — Voysey (1972) has provided some intriguing evidence and analysis — but almost nothing is known of the interaction system between the normal and the handicapped child, although their attitudes to each other have been examined (Richardson *et al.*, 1961). Systematic examination of the styles of interaction between adults and handicapped children would probably reveal some differences from the styles observed with ordinary children. Some of these differences would relate to to the nature of the disability — blindness and deafness present quite specific problems in interaction — and to the attitude system of the adults.

At the personal level it would clearly be very important to study the development of the disabled child's view of himself. The view of the self contained in such notions as self-concept, self-image, self-esteem and ideal self, would be one way of exploring the child's response to his disability, his perception of his value and status in the social systems in which he participates, and the effect of attitudes, expectations and interactions on that sense of self and its associated values. Such a study would examine topics connected with the relationship between disability and self-esteem, the effects of different socialization experiences and the association between self-concept and variables such as academic progress and career aspirations.

The study of children's self-concepts would be part of a wider search for greater understanding of personal development. It is very difficult to study this in some groups of handicapped children (we shall examine the problem in a later chapter), but we must now explore the development of the person in relation to the various social systems which influence his growth.

The forces that shape the development of a handicapped child are many. They include the nature and severity of his disability, the attitudes of those in regular contact with him and the institutions that cater for him, especially those of the home and school. In interaction these forces will affect his modes of adjustment to his handicap and the kinds and levels of skills, aptitudes and attainments that he is encouraged to acquire and develop.

While there will be significant differences at an individual level dependent upon the factors just noted, there may be elements of regularity or patterning in the children's development which are worth exploring. Of special siginificance would be the times and places causing a change in status or identity, such as the trauma of accidental handicap, the mortification of segregated schooling and the transition from the protective embrace of caring institutions to independence in society. At this stage we would need to draw upon the disabled persons' own perceptions of their childhood as well seek data through more traditional research methods. For example, the recent book by Munday (1976), a severely disabled young woman, provides valuable insights into the personal experience of disability in childhood.

There are several ways in which the study of the social psychology of disability might be approached. One method would be to see how a particular category of disability (such as epilepsy) came to acquire the social and psychological connotations it now possesses. From this point we would inquire about the public's attitudes to that disability, as well as those of professionally involved men and women. A potentially useful probe would be an examination of the social factors involved in the identification and distribution of the condition. In addition, we could explore the children's personal development within the social systems which influence it, paying special attention to the nature of their social interactions. Finally we could examine the personal world of the handicapped child and how his self-image or self-concept is affected by those around him.

To conclude this chapter, let us look at one of these areas of study — the social factors involved in identification and labelling.

Epidemiology

The study of the way in which a disability or disease is distributed in time or space (epidemiology) has provided medical science with much valuable information, especially where the origins and causes of disability are imperfectly understood. Similarly, for the social scientist findings such as the unequal distribution of a defect in children from different social classes or an unequal dsitribution between urban and rural areas can have particular significance. Data on the incidence and prevalence of the condition are essential tools for administrators and planners of medical services, the supply of speech therapists or the provision of special schools. These matters are not primarily the province of the social psychologist, although he may be concerned with the manner in which the collection of data has been influenced by social or psychological factors. To illustrate, let us take the case of researchers who, in a richly detailed study of a representative sample of school children on the Isle of Wight, found that physical handicap in children was not significantly related to social class background. They came to a broadly similar conclusion with respect to children with psychiatric disorders, but there was one anomaly. Children with asthma were much more likely to be found among those whose families could be placed in the higher social classes (Rutter, Tizard and Whitmore, 1970). The question is, is asthma a condition causally related to social class, and if so how does this happen? We could speculate that certain children in this social group are in some ways made more anxious or placed under greater stress than working-class children, and that asthma is a specific stress reaction to a particular kind of pressure. On the other hand could the epidemiological data itself be suspect? Adelstein (1976) hypothesizes that working-class children displaying similar symptoms are more likely to be labelled bronchitic rather than asthmatic. If this is so then there appears to be a social force at work which influences what appears to be objective data collection.

Epidemiology and labelling

Epidemiology involves the identification of different types of handicap, and, as the above example suggests, the categorization of disabled children may not be a totally precise or objective process. The influence of subjective elements in classification was clearly illustrated by an experiment organized by Neer in 1973, who took the well-documented association between SES and intelligence to examine the diagnostic process. Neer and his colleagues presented a group of psychologists at a guidance centre with three identical case studies, the only difference being the social background of the children. Three levels of SES were used, upper, middle and lower, and while there was no difference in the disgnoses of cases from the upper or middle classes, a highly significant difference was found in their diagnoses of children supposedly from working-class backgrounds. These were more likely to be classified as retarded than the upper- or middle-class children, even though they presented identical symptoms.

Perhaps the most vivid example of the labelling process comes from the work of Mercer (1971) who examined how children from a community in California became diagnosed as retarded. Her general and not unexpected finding was a correlation between the diagnosis of retardation and economic and ethnic factors. Using house values of above and below $10,000, 22.7 per cent of the population came from homes below this level, though they accounted for 53 per cent of the retarded. Similarly of the whole population, Anglos made up 82 per cent of the community and from this section came 54 per cent of the retarded. Mexicans represented 9.5 per cent of the community contributing 32 per cent of the retarded, while the Negro element consisted of 7 per cent of the community from which came 11 per cent of the retarded. Turning to the school system, she examined the process by which children are diagnosed as retarded and placed in special classes. The school population consisted of 80 per cent Anglos, 13 per cent Mexicans and 7 per cent Negroes. The referral rate — that is the percentage of children referred to psychologists for examination — closely followed the ethnic distribution of the school population, 82.9, 7.6 and 9.5 per cent respectively. The next stage in the process was the result of tests by the psychologists; at this stage

47.4 per cent of the Anglos were found eligible for special class placement, 32.7 per cent of the Mexicans and 19.8 of the Negro children. Following further tests, the results were converted into 'recommendation for placement in special classes' and the percentage recommended for such placement was respectively 37.9, 40.9, 21.2 per cent. Finally there was the implementation of the recommendations: 32.1 per cent of the Anglos recommended were put in special classes, 45.3 per cent of the Mexican and 22.6 per cent of the Negro children. These figures are repeated in the table below.

Table 2.2   The labelling process (Mercer 1971, p. 197)

Ethnic group	Tested by psycho-logist	Found eligible (IQ 79)	Recommen-ded for placement	Special class placement
Anglo	82.9	47.4	37.9	32.1
Mexican	7.6	32.7	40.9	45.3
Negro	9.5	19.8	21.2	22.6

The percentage of children initially tested by the psychologist was roughly similar to the distribution of ethnic groups in the community, but as the labelling-placement process continued the percentage of ethnic minority children increased, especially at the crucial point when the decision on placement was made. The percentages of Mexican and black children placed in special classes were six and two-and-a-half times larger respectively, than would have been expected by their proportionate numbers in the child population. As well as IQ and other tests, the children were given a medical examination and significant differences emerged, with Negro and Mexican children having fewer physical defects than Anglo children. This aspect could not therefore explain the over-representation of minority group children, and neither could economic factors; by far the strongest effect on placement was the ethnic background of the child.

As Mercer points out, people will explain these findings in different ways. The high incidence of disabled and retarded children from ethnic minority groups can be related to physio-logical and cognitive defects arising out of impoverishment and under-stimulating backgrounds — together with such factors as inadequate diet and inferior pre- and post-natal care. Others will see confirmation of beliefs in racial and genetic differences in the data. For Mercer a more valid perspective is to see the process as one where the 'over-representation of socio-economically disadvantaged persons and persons from ethnic minority backgrounds in the devalued status of mental retardate, can be studied as a status assignment phenomenon similar to other comparable social processes' (Mercer 1971, p.191). She also suggests that different social groups have a differential *vulnerability* to such labelling. A prime example of this vulnerability lies in the strategic importance of the IQ in the labelling process. A test standardized on the majority culture is penalizing to those from minority cultures. Consequently Mercer asks for the use of test material derived from each distinctive subculture, so that labels, such as 'retarded' would only be used when retardation was indicated by the norms of the sub-culture. This would seem a more realistic suggestion than the production of so-called culture free or culture fair tests, and indeed the revision of the Wechsler Intelligence Scale for Children Test (WISC.R) has incorporated a substantial sample of Negro children in its standardization (Wechsler, 1974).

A similar situation has been found to exist in Britain with regard to the number of immigrant children in special schools in England and Wales. In 1970-71, it was found that 5.6 per cent of immigrant children in ordinary schools came from Cyprus, Gibraltar and Malta, and they comprised some 6.1 per cent of immigrant children in special schools. Indian children made up some 20 per cent of immigrant children in ordinary schools, but only 8.3 per cent of immigrants in special schools. West Indian children represented nearly 40 per cent of immigrant children in ordinary schools and 70 per cent of such children in special schools (DES Statistics, 1972). The over-representation of West Indian children in special schools is a further example of a group vulnerable to the labelling process (Coard, 1971). But it is a phenomenon not solely confined to immigrant children; the preponderance of working-classs children in schools for the ESN is equally significant in this respect.

The concept of vulnerability to labelling is perhaps less critical in the compilation of statistics than when it becomes part of a process of assigning negative status. It can lead to what Hall (1970) has referred to as 'punitive misclassification' against which regular review and reconsideration assumes strategic importance. By themselves regular reviews will do little more than redress blatant errors of placement, and therefore it is also important to examine the organizational context in which the labelling process is carried out. Woolfe (1977) has made a more recent study of the referral procedure in a Local Educational Authority with respect to maladjusted children, and provides substantial evidence that organizational pressures can dominate clinical judgements.

3 Attitudes and the handicapped

Positive and negative attitudes

Society's attitudes place the handicapped in a subordinate status in some ways like that of ethnic minority groups (Tenny, 1953, pp.206-64). Tenny develops a common theme in rehabilitation literature that the attitudes of the majority are added encumbrances to the objective limitations of disability. The disabled person has the latter limitations, the ones imposed on him by society and the self-imposed ones that arise from accepting the status conferred by society. This static view, however, ignores the fact that attitudes towards the disabled do change.

Evolving attitudes towards the disabled and other stigmatized groups have been monitored (Pritchard, 1963; Jones, 1972; Gottlieb, 1975), and historians and social scientists provide evidence that public and professional attitudes have changed and are changing. In Britain this has been at its most rapid during the last thirty years. We can regard the press, television and the persuasive power of voluntary societies as important in this connection (Nightingale, 1973). Pilkington (1973) has chronicled the impact of television on reactions to mental illness and mental handicap, though research is needed so far as other handicaps are concerned.

Legal changes and new concepts of help, care and support reinforce the conclusion that during this period a more tolerant and understanding attitude towards various kinds of disability has developed. However, despite these positive gains there is still a residue of uncertainty, mistrust and downright discrimination against which the disabled have to contend.

Public attitudes vary according to perceptions of the nature, severity and prognosis of disabilities as well as according to the age of the disabled person — it appears that handicapped children suffer less in this respect than adults, and attitudes towards any type of disability will range from indifference to hostility. These attitudes are reflected in personal encounters as well as in the discrimination implicit in certain legal or administrative restraints. Whilst it is valid to compare the disabled with ethnic minority groups (both suffer social distancing and marginality, negative portrayal in literature and humour, segregated schooling and vocational disadvantages), the analogy must not be pushed too far. The black child may experience negative social attitudes from an early age, but the disabled child can be protected during childhood from their full force. The family with a handicapped child does not automatically share his devalued social status, but black children and their families have a collective burden. Whilst attitudes vary with the perception of the disability, colour can be a uniform stigma. One other very important difference is that the disabled are not seen as a social threat — property values do not drop if a person in a wheelchair moves into a neighbourhood (though the setting up of a hostel for the retarded can arouse community opposition).

An attitude (and there are many definitions) represents both 'an orientation towards or away from some object, concept, or situation and a readiness to respond in a pre-determined manner to these, or related objects, concepts or situations' (Hilgard and Atkinson, 1967, p.583). Orientations and responses have intellectual and emotional components, and the basis of any particular attitude towards an individual or group may be well understood by the person who holds it or it may reside at an unconscious level. Attitudes are learned in various ways: the attitudes of those who hold key positions in our lives can be internalized; personal and distinctive attitudes can be acquired from particular personal circumstances or from a single traumatic event or, without serious reflection, from the general social surroundings. Some attitudes are so firmly embedded that they can be legitimately regarded as stable elements of the personality, vigorously resistant to modification.

Sarnoff, Katz and McClintock (1970, p.168) suggest that attitudes and their formation can be interpreted in terms of the psychological functions that they fulfil. Man is a creative being, attempting to make sense of his world and his experience — a process they describe as a 'search after meaning'. Attitudes can be seen as a function of the 'range of information which has been accessible to an individual in regard to certain target objects'. Negative attitudes to minority groups may grow out of limited and biased knowledge or hearsay; these are open to change by the receipt of additional knowledge. Attitudes arise from the pressure of group membership, where through the selective use of rewards and punishment the group encourages the expression of attitudes consonant with its value system. Rejection of group attitudes can lead to 'social ostracism', but the support the individual gives them will depend on his need for group membership. Attitudes may function as a form of ego-defence and they they may be compared with symptoms. Racial bigotry is a symptom of hostile impulses projected on to others; the bigot 'gains gratification of his impulses while maintaining the fiction that the impulses originate in others rather than himself' (Sarnoff *et al.*, 1970, p.169). Attitudes may develop in these three motivational contexts — the search for meaning, group conformity and ego needs — and the more psychologically profound the basis for an attitude, the more resistant it is to change.

The extreme form of negative attitude is prejudice, which is, as Klineberg (1968) noted, a state reached before relevant data have been collected and examined. Prejudice has its conceptual-intellectual component (ideas and opinions about groups or persons), its attitudinal component (positive or negative attitudes and the ascribing of positive or negative values to others as well as the emotional colouring of these attitudes), and a conative one which is a disposition to behave and act in accordance with the other components. The conceptual component of prejudice is expressed in the use of stereotypes — the attributing of self-selected characteristics to human groups. Stereotyping has been elegantly described as the 'relation between a set of attributes which vary on continuous dimensions and classifications which are discontinuous' (Tajfel, 1969, pp.177-8). Human skin colour, for example, ranges from white through to brown and to black, with many fine gradations, yet racists talk and behave as though this continuous dimension, colour, yielded to a simple twofold classification of black or white. For Tajfel the significance of this component of prejudice for a person is that it produces the semblance of order. Since human beings and human nature are not orderly, it is easier to accept pre-judgements rather than have them upset. He notes that in the absence of specific data there will be a tendency to 'ascribe to an individual the characteristics which we derive from our knowledge of his class membership' and that in ambiguous social situations it is easier to find data which support suppositions based on clan membership than to seek evidence which contradicts it. Making such judgements at a distance allows little or none of the negative feedback that is more likely in face-to-face encounters. Of course, challenge does not mean change, since the prejudiced person 'has an emotional investment in preserving the differentiations between his group and others' (Tajfel, 1969, p.181).

Prejudiced views are acquired through the assimilation process involved in the learning of evaluations and preferences in one's childhood, identification with one's own social group and the acceptance of that group's evaluation of other groups. This is partly to do with the relative status of one social group as against another. The status of groups is subject to change — as shown by the changing status of immigrant groups in the United States — and faced with declining social status a group may seek to explain this by attributing negative values to ascending groups and to develop self-supportive ideologies within the threatened group.

Attitudes towards the handicapped presumably follow the lines of attitude formation suggested by Sarnoff, the negative, prejudiced attitudes the process discussed by Tajfel. If, as noted earlier, there is evidence that attitudes to the handicapped have become more humane, then this may be because the original negative ones were largely the result of ignorance and misinformation and were modified by education or other sources of information. How certain individuals develop highly positive attitudes towards groups which are otherwise stigmatized is a matter of great interest, but one with which we cannot deal fully here.

Social distance and the handicapped

One well-established procedure for estimating attitudes to other
nationals or minority groups is that devised by Bogardus (1925) and
known as social distance. This measures the degree of intimacy at
which a person would be at ease with another. A similar procedure
has been used with the handicapped. An individual does not need
to have personal knowledge of members of other groups in order to
hold an attitude towards them. Jones, Gottfried and Owens (1966)
found that the non-handicapped could show their preferences for
different kinds of disability without any direct contact. Shears and
Jensema (1969, p.95) invited 94 normal adults to rank ten disabilities in order of severity — both as disabilities in themselves and as
disabilities in a friend (see Table 3.1). The rank order (the lower the
rank — 10 being the lowest and worst — the greater the perception
of disadvantage) for 'self' shows that the loss of a limb is regarded
as less serious than retardation or homosexuality. The rank order for
'friend' reveals some differences — blindness, for example, is more
acceptable in a friend than in self.

Table 3.1   Rank ordering of anomalies for self and friend

'Friend'		'Self'	
Anomaly	*Mean rank*	*Anomaly*	*Mean rank*
1. Amputee	1.99	Amputee	2.25
2. Blind	2.72	Stutterer	2.57
3. Wheelchair	2.76	Hare-lip	2.71
4. Hare-lip	3.56	Wheelchair	3.52
5. Stutterer	3.81	Blind	4.52
6. Deaf-mute	4.89	Deaf-mute	4.54
7. Cerebral palsied	6.07	Mentally ill	5.90
8. Mentally ill	6.42	Cerebral palsied	6.49
9. Retarded	6.69	Homosexual	6.63
10. Homosexual	7.44	Retarded	7.18

The subjects were then asked about social settings of increasing
intimacy. As can be seen from Table 3.2 (Shears and Jensema,
1969, p.93) the percentage of acceptance decreases as the level of
intimacy rises. But the percentages are not uniform: the greater the
severity or stigma of the handicap, the lower the percentage of

acceptance. Shears and Jensema abstracted three groups: (a) amputee, wheelchair person and blind; (b) deaf, speech-handicapped and stutterer, and (c) mentally ill, retarded and homosexual — the cerebral palsied person occupied a position mid-way between groups (b) and (c). In explaining the difference in attitudes revealed by the social distance measure, they postulate that disabilities with a high measure of acceptance are visible and associated with stereotypes, and those with low acceptance are associated with stigma. The conditions in an intermediate position are the ones which cause problems in interpersonal communication.

If interactional awkwardness is a factor affecting social distance, then the visibly handicapped give anticipatory cues for the non-handicapped which allow them to prepare for social encounters, while the deaf and speech-handicapped, who do not provide this anticipatory period, present particular unavoidable communication problems in encounters. Shears and Jensema concluded that social acceptance was probably based on six factors: visibility of affliction, interference with the communication process, social stigma, prognosis, extent of incapacity and degree of difficulty in adjusting to daily life.

A somewhat similar investigation was carried out by Semmel and Dickson (1966) into the cognitive and emotional associations of

Table 3.2   Percentage of subjects who would accept certain anomalous persons in specific situations

Anomaly	Would marry	Would have as friend	Would work with	Would live in same neighbourhood	Would speak to	Would live in same country
Amputee	18.18	79.79	90.90	95.95	98.98	100
Wheelchair	7.21	79.38	92.78	97.93	98.96	100
Blind	16.12	77.41	89.24	95.69	100	100
Hare-lip	8.24	69.07	80.41	87.62	98.97	98.97
Stutterer	7.14	65.30	74.48	83.67	96.93	100
Deaf-mute	10.41	53.12	66.66	80.20	94.79	100
Cerebral palsied	1.03	38.14	50.51	65.97	88.65	100
Retarded	00.00	23.95	30.20	54.16	86.45	100
Mentally ill	2.10	28.42	37.39	45.26	70.52	97.89
Homosexual	1.01	17.17	27.27	45.45	71.71	98.98

particular disability labels (blind, cerebral-palsied, deaf, epileptic, mentally retarded, normal negro and stutterer). They asked a group of college students to indicate their reactions to these disabilities by noting the degree to which they would feel 'comfortable', 'indifferent' or 'uncomfortable' in the presence of a disabled person in ten 'situational contexts', e.g. dating, having a meal with, sharing a room with, working alongside, etc. The college students included 345 who were majoring in education, and 112 majoring in special education. The investigators found that during the course of college training there was little significant change in the connotative meanings attached to disability labels, although the special education majors continued to hold more positive attitudes than the other students. However, statistically significant differences were found between the students' various connotative reactions. The most favourable responses to the disability labels were given in the following order: normal white, stutterer, deaf, blind, normal negro, epileptic, mentally retarded and cerebral-palsied. These responses were significantly influenced by the 'situational context': the more permanent and intimate contexts evoked less favourable connotations than those indicating more ephemeral and socially distant interactions with the disabled persons.

Attitudes: a cultural phenomenon

The belief that attitudes towards handicaps can be, as it were, built into the culture, receives support from a number of sources. One is the examination by Haffter (1968) of the history of attitudes. His basic material was folktales from Western Europe which he used to explore changes in popular attitudes to childhood disability. He saw that one constant theme in these tales, some of them dating back to the Middle Ages, was that of the changeling. The normal child is exchanged for one who is badly proportioned or crippled or mute. The folk tales were explanatory devices by which a peasant society could understand the phenomenon of hydrocephalic or retarded children. Alongside the tale was a body of folk wisdom for getting rid of the deformed infant (exposure, beating, drowning, etc.). They illustrate the belief in the Middle Ages that the handicapped child was 'not a human creature at all but a subhuman one, ... surreptitiously substituted for the real child shortly after birth' (Haffter, 1968, p.57).

With the spread of Christianity the nature of the explanations changes and far from the changeling being seen as a misfortune, demons were invoked and the impiety or misconduct of the parents became the cause of the birth of a deformed infant. In some parts of Europe deformity in the newly-born was adequate evidence of involvement in witchcraft; this in turn led to the concealment of many handicapped children. As Haffter points out, these beliefs persisted in remote regions long after they were abandoned by better-educated communities, and he notes that one of the last recorded cases of the tormenting of a changeling occurred as late as 1895. The transformation of the idea of the changeling by Christian demonology meant that the existence of the child was a public denouncement of the parents' actions and even their thoughts. 'It ... became a shameful stigma in the eyes of society and a reason for isolation, ostracism and even presecution' (Haffter, 1968, pp.60-1). He goes further than perhaps many of us would when he suggests that a residue of these earlier beliefs actually influences present-day attitudes through a societal 'collective unconscious', but it would be rash to claim that the beliefs have been totally eradicated even in technologically advanced societies.

Anthropology might provide insight into the development of attitudes in our own past. Hanks and Hanks (1948), examining attitudes to disability in non-Western cultures, found that Western concepts of disability could not easily be used as ethnological data since what was seen as a handicap in one non-Western culture was not in another. Considering the social status of those who were viewed as handicapped in their own culture, they concluded that one can categorize social attitudes about the rights and obligations of the dominant group to the afflicted, and the meanings attached to the symptoms — which can have mystical or magical associations.

When the social status of the afflicted was at its lowest, Hanks and Hanks called this as *pariah status*, the afflicted having no rights to seek or claim help and being seen by the majority as a threat. In cultures where disability reduces people's capacity to hunt or gather food, stringent measures may be taken to remove this *economic liability*; they give examples of this practice among the Eskimos. An improved status was enjoyed by the disabled in cultures which practiced a *tolerant utilization*, where the person was expected to contribute to his tribe or clan insofar as he was able, and his involvement in social life was limited only by his ability and inclination — this was apparently the case among certain North American Indian tribes. Other cultures allowed the disabled a strictly *limited participation* — they clearly defined the rights and obligations of the disabled but these were more circumscribed than those of the active majority. Finally, Hanks and Hanks noted that in parts of East Africa the handicapped enjoyed a *laissez-faire* social status. Here they were given shelter and protection and there was no obligation or even covert pressure on them to contribute to the group; the definition of achievement was broad and it was possible for the handicapped to gain a measure of prestige and status by exercising such abilities as they had, though there was no pressure on them to do so.

This study also showed the wide variety of explanations offered for the existence of disability — as the consequence of behaviour in a previous existence, or of the loss of the protection of supernatural powers, or of sorcery or the breach of tribal taboos. The authors saw a connection between prevailing attitudes and social and economic factors, and concluded that

> ... protection of the physically handicapped and social particip-ation for them is increased where: (1) the level of productivity is higher in proportion to the population and its distribution more nearly equal; (2) competitive factors in individual or group achievement are minimized; (3) the criteria of achievement are less formally absolute as in hierarchical social structures and more weighted with concern for individual capacity, as in democratic social structures'. (Hanks and Hanks, 1948, p.20)

The relationship between attitudes to disability and a society's economic wealth has been confirmed by Jordan and Friesen (1969). They examined attitudes and socio-economic development in Columbia, Peru and the United States and found progressively more positive attitudes to disability as the economic status of the country improved. Before congratulating ourselves on our superior attitudes we might reflect that it not necessarily personal virtue but fortunate circumstances that may account for the improvement in current attitudes.

Culture-wide attitudes

The examination of attitudes in cultures different from our own leads to the question whether there is a set of attitudes towards disability and handicap — or are attitudes a matter of individual preference and experience? In a series of researches Richardson and his colleagues (1961) have explored this question. Using a simple and elegant technique (showing to children and adults drawings of handicapped children and asking them to rank the pictures in order of preference), they apparently reveal the existence of uniform attitudes towards handicap. The drawings consisted of A — child with no handicap; L — child with crutches and a brace on the left left; W — child in a wheelchair; H — child with left hand missing; F — child with a facial disfigurement; and O — an obese child. Children from a wide range of social and geographical backgrounds, also including handicapped children, ranked the drawings. Six sub-samples of children ranked the pictures in the same order — A, L, W, H, F and O, i.e. the normal child first and the obese child last. Table 3.3 shows this startling conformity (with the minor exception of the Puerto Rican group for whom the rank order of W and H is reversed).

Richardson suggested that boys, who might be more concerned with physical activity, would rate functional disabilities lower and that girls, being more concerned with social relationships, would react strongly against handicaps such as facial disfigurement and obesity. The rank order A, L, W, H, F, O, was found in both boys and girls but there *was* a tendency for boys and girls to react in that way. Perhaps the most surprising result was that both the handicapped and the non-handicapped expressed the same attitudes. To explain this, Richardson advanced several views, e.g. that the rankings reflect functional impairment (though the low ranking of the obese child does not support this); that facial characteristics dominate impressions — there is support for this given in the low ranking of F; and that the uniform first ranking of drawing A could be explained by a preference for the familiar rather than the unfamiliar.

The uniformity of response by the handicapped and non-handicapped is explained by minority cultures absorbing the values of the majority, and the uniformity across social and ethnic groups

Table 3.3   Rank position of drawings for the various subgroups

Rank position	Total	Sex		Disability	
		Boys	Girls	Handi-capped	Non-handi-capped
1	A	A	A	A	A
2	L	L	L	L	L
3	W	W	W	W	W
4	H	H	H	H	H
5	F	F	F	F	F
6	O	O	O	O	O
N	640	317	323	144	496

Rank position	Race			Urban-Rural		
	White	Negro	Puerto-Rican	Urban	Sub-urban	Rural
1	A	A	A	A	A	A
2	L	L	L	L	L	L
3	W	W	H	W	W	W
4	H	H	W	H	H	H
5	F	F	F	F	F	F
6	O	O	O	O	O	O
N	351	183	104	423	104	113

Rank position	Socio-economic status		Setting	
	Low	Middle and upper	Camp	School
1	A	A	A	A
2	L	L	L	L
3	W	W	W	W
4	H	H	H	H
5	F	F	F	F
6	O	O	O	O
N	559	104	381	259

Table 3.4   Preference rankings of handicaps by sex

Males	Rank order						
Grade	A	L	W	H	F	O	No. of subjects
Kindergarten	2	4	5	3	1	6	53
1	1	4	6	3	2	5	51
2	1	4	6	3	2	5	48
3	1	4	6	3	2	5	53
4	1	4	5	3	2	6	49
5	1	3	5	4	2	6	67
6	1	3	5	6	2	4	59
7	1	3	5	6	2	4	55
9	1	2	5	6	3	4	56
12	1	2.5	2.5	6	4	5	39
Parents	1	2	3	6	4	5	87

by the gradual exposure of children to 'depreciatory evaluations of persons with physical disabilities'. Advertising exploits 'cultural stereotypes of physical beauty which are identified with goodness'. The converse is that children are also exposed to more positive images of disability (through television and posters). Richardson concluded that this study has shown a consistent preference among all subgroups for the non-handicapped; a consistent ordering of disabilities by children from different backgrounds; and a consistent preference for certain types of disability.

In a subsequent study, Richardson (1970, p.209) examined the the age at which this consistent preference emerged. The same drawings were shown to children aged 5-12, 13, 15 and 18 and samples of parents ranked the pictures as they thought a 10 or 11 year-old boy or girl would (see Table 3.4). The results revealed that by age 5 or 6 group values are emerging and that an orderly change in them through adolescence leads to children and parents eventually sharing the same values. Among the 6-8-year-olds, disabled children are rejected because they do not fulfil expectations. The more the drawing differs in overall appearance from the normal, the lower the ranking. With older children, especially girls, facial disfigurement appears to influence judgement, suggesting that with increasing maturity it is the social meanings of disability that influences the ranking process. One of the findings — the low ranking of the obese child — is because (a) for younger children he presents an image physically different from the norm, and (b) for the older children obesity is not only socially unacceptable, but obese children are held to be *responsible* for their condition.

In general the Richardson findings indicate a gradual assimilation of group values that are consistent across social background, age, sex and disability.

Such uniformity of response is unlikely. Uniform attitudes seem so unlikely that we need to scrutinize the procedure used, in order to eliminate any possibility of the findings being influenced by the drawings — are they similar except for the presence of disability? Those employed by Richardson show that care was taken over this, and only with the child with a facial disfigurement is there any ambiguity about the artist's intention. Then we can consider the way in which the children attempted the task: they were told, 'Look at all these pictures. Tells me which boy (or girl) you like best'. The subject pointed to a picture which was then removed. 'Which boy (or girl) do you like next best?' (*sic*). Here we may have some doubts, for we have no way of knowing how children interpret 'like best' — nor do we know whether they have actually seen the disability element in the drawing. But they do interpret the instructions and however they scan the drawings, the results are remarkably consistent. But is this consistency a statistical construct? Each child's ranking of the pictures is added to the others from his group to obtain an average, and it is these average rankings which are the basis of the uniformity. It is theoretically possible for the average group rankings to be as they are without a single individual child ranking the pictures in that order.

Richardson supplies evidence of the high level of agreement in ranking within groups. But this is not necessarily the same as saying that many children (as individuals) provide rankings identical to the group average. It might be argued that group average rankings are useful as indicators of group values but one cannot determine the extent to which this is reflected in individual preferences. Similarly, Richardson assumes that differences in average rankings are meaningful, but from his published data there is no way of calculating this since standard deviations are nor supplied — it could be that simple and minor differences are not statistically significant. The concept of 'cultural uniformity' is acceptable only insofar as the average ranks are held to be expressive of group perceptions. The extent to which individuals display similar values remains to be shown in their rankings. An alternative treatment would be to report the most frequently occurring ranking preferences, but clearly the degree of individual variation in response will need to be examined further. The assumption that the rank order of pictures represents an equal interval scale could easily be tested empirically, as could reliability data (which are not given). Preliminary work with English children (both normal and handicapped) suggests that even if cultural conformity can be shown to exist, cross-cultural conformity is even more problematic.

Richardson suggests that in the acquiring of attitudes and values about disability there is at work a subtle, non-conscious learning process by which groups 'agree'. This seems to be non-controversial although details of the process remain obscure. But there are also attitudes which appear to be part of the individual's personality and to a lesser extent influenced by cultural norms.

Attitudes and personality

We have already discussed Sarnoff's thesis that prejudice can be linked with ego needs and ego weakness. There have been a few studies of the relationship between personality and attitudes to disability. One view is that a person with strong negative attitudes to one minority group may well display similar attitudes to other disadvantaged groups. Chesler (1965) devised a measure of 'ethno-centrism' and compared responses on this measure with expressed attitudes to a non-ethnic minority group — the disabled. Using four dimensions of ethnocentrism (race, religion, nationality and social class) he found that negative attitudes to one group correlated with negative attitudes to other groups. Those who showed high ethno-centrism or marked rejection of 'out-groups' also expressed negative attitudes towards the disabled.

The relationship between personality and attitudes towards the disabled has been clarified by Noonan, Barry and Davis (1970). Their assumption was that attitudes are influenced by selective personality variables, and they compared college students' responses on a number of personality tests with their responses to two measures of attitudes towards disability. These two measures were called criterion measures, and consisted of the Attitude Towards Disabled Persons test (ATDP) by Yuker, Block and Cambell (1960) and an unpublished projective test involving ambiguous illustrations of visibly disabled persons who were depicted in twelve scenes of social interaction. Subjects were invited to write brief stories about each picture. The results obtained from the criterion measures were systematically compared with the results from the personality tests. These personality tests included measurements of cultural conformity (the extent to which a person conforms to prevailing beliefs), of ego strength, of authoritarianism, the degree of conscious bodily satisfaction, degree of unconscious concern about one's own body, and field independence. This last measurement referred here to a belief that the visibly disabled do not conform to our image of what a person should look like, and that the contrast between experience and expectation might lead to anxiety and hostility. It was hypothesized that this conceptual frame of reference would be detectable in the subject's performance in the test of visual perception used in the study.

As well as examining the statistical relationship between the criterion measures and personality tests, the investigators also included a check on the extent to which subjects were simply giving responses they thought socially acceptable. Among the personality measures unaffected by the social desirability factor and strongly associated with attitudes towards the visibly disabled, was authoritarianism. The greater the degree of authoritarianism, the more negative and aversive was the reaction to visible disability. The interaction between different personality measures was also assessed. Thus when authoritarianism was accompanied by low ego strength, the earlier relationship was found to be even more significant, as stronger negative attitudes towards disability were expressed. In attempting to explain this finding, the authors suggested that an authoritarian person sees the disabled as a minority group provoking 'avoidance, discomfort and contempt' in those who wish to be associated with the powerful, successful and influential members of our society.

It is premature to suggest that these findings, if confirmed, could be applied in practice in personnel selection, but in the future it might be worth considering whether attitude measures could form part of the selection process for key positions in rehabilitation or special education.

So far we have discussed two views about attitudes towards handicap — a global, societal one involving the incorporation of ideas and opinions embedded in a community as a form of non-conscious ideology, and one that regards the attitudes as an aspect of the personality somewhat independent of these broad social trends. The nature of social encounters between the handicapped and non-handicapped provides a link between them.

Social encounters

It is a major theme in rehabilitation literature that physical handicap elicits a negative response from other people. Goffman suggests that certain physical characteristics with negative values are responsible for the behaviour in face-to-face encounters in which the disabled person is at a disadvantage. When normal and stigmatized meet there is, in his terms, 'one of the primal scenes of sociology ... the moment ... where the cause and effects of stigma must be directly confronted by both sides' (Goffman, 1968, p.24). Attitudes towards the handicapped stem either from an implicit form of social learning or from the personality of the individual, and it is possible that the problems of handling interpersonal encounters are a contributory factor.

The evidence of interpersonal difficulties comes from three sources — interviews with handicapped persons, social psychological experiments, and the autobiographies of the handicapped.

Davis (1964) used evidence given by handicapped persons in order to examine face-to-face interaction — especially initial encounters — which he refers to as the zone of *first impressions*. His subjects were people with a visible disability, and from his interviews he concludes that the pattern of social encounters contains the following elements. Any awkwardness in the initial encounter denies the disabled person his preferred social identity — physically different but socially normal. There may be awkwardness because the non-handicapped is inexperienced in communicating with the handicapped, or is uncertain of his attitudes and is burdened with the stereotyped expectations. One facet of awkwardness is that social behaviour, at least towards those we are meeting for the first time, requires a wide spectrum of attention, but this is limited by the obtrusiveness of a disability. Great care taken to avoid glancing at, or mentioning, a disability can make it the focal point of an encounter. Another source of awkwardness is the normal person's uncertainty of the extent to which emotion can be expressed: must he conceal feelings of pity?

Will he be able to hide feelings of repugnance?

Awkwardness also arises because sometimes the disabled and non-disabled aspects of the handicapped person are felt to be incongruous. Davis quotes one subject's report of someone saying, 'How strange that someone so pretty should be in a wheelchair' (Davis, 1964, p.125). Conversation may be inhibited by the normal person's uncertainty of the extent to which the disabled one knows about and can take part in general social activities (going to the theatre, etc.), and for each interactional puzzle for the normal there is the 'counter enigma' for the handicapped.

The process of 'getting to know' is analysed by Davis as passing through three stages. First there is *fictionalized acceptance* — where the disabled is given surface acceptance, and the interaction is kept to the minimum necessary for conventional politeness. If the potential relationship is to develop, the visibly handicapped may have to be hostile to this and to discourage it as a basis for a deeper relationship, but at least it allows a marginal denial of deviancy. Beyond this stage is the 'breaking through' process — helping *normalized role-taking* — where the disability and its constraints are admitted into the context of the relationship and, as the latter develops, the visibility of the affliction becomes less central. In essence both parties are engaged in reciprocal role-taking and both are unconstrained by previous uncertainties. In the third stage — *institutionalization of normal relationships* — having lost the imputation of deviance, the disabled has to deal with the reality that his disability does limit his range of social responses. That is, he has to 'integrate effectively a major claim to "normalcy" with numerous minor waivers of the same claim (and this is a tricky feat) ... ', again for both parties (Davis, 1964, p.132).

Davis argues (correctly) that the behavioural constraints on both parties are similar to other kinds of interactional awkwardness with which we are familiar. There is difference of degree, not of kind.

Several of the points discussed by Davis have been confirmed experimentally. Kleck (1966) examined the behaviour of subjects towards a research confederate posing as a disabled person in a wheelchair. The investigation was particularly concerned with eye-to-eye contact, movements of the body and head, impression formation (subjects' rating of the confederate for traits such as 'friendly-unfriendly') and opinion distortion (whether subjects concealed their true opinions when with a disabled person). Their behaviour with the 'disabled' confederate and with a non-disabled one were compared. Eye-to-eye contacts with the 'disabled' were not significantly different from those with the normal confederate, though the subjects were more inhibited in their movements, did form more positive views of the 'disabled' person and modified their views on sport and politics in ways they thought would be consistent with his — e.g. appearing less in favour of sport when with him.

The experimental situation is similar to Davis's zone of first impressions, during which eye-to-eye contacts are maintained (to avoid looking directly at the disability?), while movement is inhibited because of anxiety or uncertainty. The opinion distortion is, as Kleck suggests, part of a desire to be kind to the handicapped. The positive evaluation of the personality of the 'disabled' confederate may be due to initial low expectations being destroyed by his conversational ability. In general, the experiment confirms some of Davis's views about awkwardness in initial encounters. If brief encounters, rather than sustained relationships, are the typical experience of handicapped people, then continuous exposure to such stress, anxiety and uncertainty in which real opinions are not shared hardly makes for normal role-taking.

The third source comes from the account disabled people have given of their experiences — accounts such as Christy Brown's *My Left Foot* (1954) and Garland Minton's *Blind Man's Buff* (1974), confirm several of the views of Davis and findings of Kleck. It seems that many of the negative attitudes referred to in the literature can be ascribed to problems of interaction. The awkwardness and discomfort so often discussed would in itself account for avoidance and rejection. Unless a non-handicapped person is highly motivated to sustain a relationship with a handicapped one, the cost may be too great for anything more than fictionalized acceptance.

Attitudes to specific handicaps

There is little doubt that attitudes vary according to the nature of the disability, although their variety may have just a single source (Jones, 1974). In chapter 1 we categorized disabilities as visible, presenting difficulties of communication, episodic, stigmatized or as some combination of these. Let us examine the varying attitudes towards blindness, epilepsy and mental retardation — representing visual, episodic and stigmatizing conditions, respectively.

Lukoff notes that a common complaint of people who are blind is that they are not treated as people — instead 'this handicap seems to arouse very special attitudes reserved for the blind' (Lukoff *et al.*, 1972, p.1). Thus blindness dominates interactions. Attitudes, whether in terms of institutional provision, difficulties of access to public places, or everyday contact seem to be of a particular kind. They may be negative or, even when there is no prejudice, they may still seem to the blind to 'colour' social contacts.

Lukoff traces the evolution of attitudes towards blindness — from neglect and hostility to compassion. The paradox is that the pity aroused by this comprehensible handicap is something with which independent blind persons have to contend. Among them are those who resent the inadequacy imputed by the offer of a helping hand, or who are not content with the lifestyle designed for them by specific institutions. 'It is the blind who insist on thrusting themselves into society, who want to broaden their economic and social basis, who make us conscious of their attitudes to blindness' (Lukoff, 1972, p.4).

Lukoff challenges the views that in social interactions there are pervasive attitudes to blind people. Instead he suggests that attitudes are differentiated — for example, one may pity and also avoid, or pity and seek to meet — and that there are unrealistic expectations on both sides of the sighted-blind divide. One of the major sources of difficulty is the 'relative lack of any guiding norms for situations where blind and sighted first encounter each other ... ' (p.8). He found that among the sighted there was a readiness to 'help' the blind (even without clear signals for that need) and a tendency towards more protective and patronizing attitudes, and of course it is from such factors that the blind form their opinion of the sighted.

Lukoff stresses the distinction between generalized public attitudes towards blindness, and the 'enduring social relationships' that influence the blind person's concept of himself. The general attitudes, 'patronizing, overly sentimental, overly protective', are seen as less significant than those of families, friends, educators and employers, and it is the attitudes of this more immediate group that determine the degree of independence from, or of conformity to, the role of blind person. He is not simply a mirror reflecting and internalizing these attitudes, he is an active agent in shaping them — by acting a compliant role or energetically offering an alternative definition of self, sometimes aggressively so. But it is those persons, roles and institutions in contact with the blind person which have the greatest impact in 'shaping how he formulates for himself his notions of the kind of person he is ...' (p.11). The ways of lessening pressure towards isolation or the acceptance of dependence are much closer to home than to a very generalized public, and for the changing of attitudes it is the area 'close to home' that requires immediate attention. It is here that the fundamental belief that the blind person is normal but blind, and not occupying a blind role, is acquired and reinforced.

Lukoff believes that the blind are learning to become more effective managers of social encounters and that this encourages a view of them as people, not as objects of pity; however, there is room for further work in this area, since some blind people are socially clumsy and this encourages the sighted to avoid the blind generally. Legislative and institutional developments must parallel increased natural acceptance at the interpersonal level so that the blind can have full access to all community roles other than those excluded by their physical limitation.

The history of the social progress of the blind offers many valuable lessons. We have witnessed in the last century a move away from ostracism to over-protection, and the latter is incompatible with the growth of valid independence for the blind. Indeed the special attitudes aroused by blindness may be more intransigent than overtly discriminating ones. If we accept Lukoff's views of the importance of those close to the blind person, then parental skills should involve more than child management, and should help foster an independent self-concept in the blind child — a process which should be continued at school.

Turning to *epilepsy*, Harrison (1976, p.498) suggests that a 'Key sociological question is: what do those who suffer from epilepsy fear from being perceived as, or labelled "epileptic"?' Epilepsy is a term covering a wide range of conditions from a momentary loss of awareness to the public image of the *grand mal* — unconsciousness, writhing limbs and incontinence. It is a symptom, not a disease, arising from a number of causes. One child in twenty suffers one convulsion during childhood. A smaller proportion have more severe symptoms; for some the symptoms may disappear with treatment or spontaneously, whilst for others they become chronic. Many beliefs still persist that are relics of beliefs about being possessed or about a link between epilepsy, mental illness and retardation.

Harrison explored the experiences of a sample of people with epilepsy now in the 20- to 30-year age group. In interviews he noted that memories of childhood convulsions were vague or were considered, even by those with long-standing convulsive disorders, as 'occasional blackouts' — that is, the convulsions were explained or handled by using forgetfulness or socially acceptable euphemisms, which were perhaps a measure of the anxiety they had aroused. Even where the epilepsy was controlled or had not reappeared for many years, victims expressed their deep worries about possible exposure: ' ... even after a lapse of 15 years our research accidentally reawakens the fear that something dreadful inside has remained, and she asked if we could arrange a fresh consultation so that she could discover "the truth".' Harrison noted that considerable anxiety arose from the patient not being fully informed on the nature of the symptoms, treatment or prognosis; without this some patients invent their own explanations.

Harrison considered that a useful framework for studying epilepsy is Goffman's theory of stigma — the relationship between an attribute and the stereotype. Almost by definition an episodic symptom like epilepsy makes the epileptic 'discreditable'. People with epilepsy avoid being 'discreditable' in various ways: by not having 'real epilepsy'; by denying it altogether, as one man did who only had nocturnal seizures (though he continued to take medication); or by concealing it from those who have 'the power to diminish one's life chances', especially employers. Disclosure has to be handled with tact — both with employers and colleagues.

Harrison noted that as well as those who were conscious of their own and others' attitudes, there was a small group of epileptics with diminished mental capacity who were oblivious to the attitudes of others. A third group accepted the image of epilepsy, and lifelong sufferers did not mention it as one of the illnesses of childhood. It had become a taken-for-granted aspect of their 'identity'. The study examined the perception of adult epileptics reflecting on their childhood experiences and as such, it represents an authentic 'inside' view, but of course the sample is talking about the attitudes and conditions of 15 to 20 years ago. Do today's epileptic children feel the same? Harrison concludes that prejudice against epilepsy is understandable since it is 'an awful thing to have'.

Blindness, we have seen, produces a special kind of response; epilepsy appears to evoke both care and pity, and shuddering avoidance. Also, the epileptic is psychologically threatened by potential discovery and loss of the dignity associated with control over one's actions.

Retardation is a term more notable for what it conceals than what it reveals. It covers persons with chromosomal defects such as Down's syndrome, those with damaged central nervous systems, and those with unknown disorders, but they all share a low level of mental or social functioning. It refers to both children and adults who, considered as a class or group, show a remarkable range of abilities and disabilities. For some the label of 'retarded' or 'subnormal' means that they have failed to cope with certain social or educational demands at a particular time. For others the status lasts throughout life.

Gottlieb (1975, p.102) notes that available studies of community attitudes to the retarded person show many inconsistencies, but he sums up that 'the predominant view of mental retardation among the public at large is that of a mongoloid or physically damaged person'. Moreover, though most of the retarded are those whose difficulties are due to cultural or environmental factors and not to genetic or observable organic defects, this view is deeply embedded in community consciousness and presumably very resistant to change. Gottwald (1970) found that in a large sample respondents made little or no attempt to discriminate between different *levels* of retardation — the label evoked a simple and derogatory stereotype. The effects of asking different kinds of attitude questions are shown by Jaffe (1966), who found that the label 'mentally retarded' was perceived more unfavourably and more variably than a sketch of the retarded person, and as Gottlieb points out, response may vary more when the stimulus is made more complex, e.g. by showing a video-recording or actually meeting a retarded person. Much of the variability in reported attitudes is clearly due to researchers using the label 'retarded' — this allows the respondent to construct his own meaning for the term; when distinctions are drawn between the severer and the milder forms, distinct attitude differences emerge in the expected direction.

Among the variables studied as associated with attitudes are the subjects' age, sex, educational level, socio-economic status, and degree of contact with the retarded (Jaffe, 1966, p.106). Though the evidence is not clear-cut there is support for the belief that women express more favourable attitudes than men, and with some exceptions, younger subjects express more positive attitudes towards the mentally retarded than older persons. The relationship between educational levels and attitudes is unclear — some studies show higher education to be linked with positive attitudes, and others the reverse. It is the same with socio-economic status since there does not appear to be a set of consistent class-linked attitudes.

Of considerable interest is the effect of contact with the retarded since it has been thought that interaction will lead to more positive and accepting attitudes. Gottlieb quotes a study by Cleland and Chambers (1959) on the impact of taking students on a tour of an institution for the retarded. Attitudes were assessed before and after the visit. Afterwards the students expressed more favourable attitudes though they were more likely than before to approve of institutionalization. Begab (1968) studied the effect of instruction and contact on the attitudes of social work students and found that they did become more positive, but only marginally.

The acceptance of retarded children by their non-retarded peers in the classroom has been the subject of many studies. Gottlieb (1975) summarizes them as suggesting that irrespective of organizational context — special classes or integrated settings — retarded children are less frequently chosen as 'best friend' or 'who you would like to play with' in sociometric investigations than ordinary children. However, studies of children's attitudes using *other* than sociometric measures (e.g. Clark, 1964, who obtained descriptions of retarded children known best by classmates) show that not all retarded children are rejected or perceived unfavourably.

Lukoff made the point that it is not generally held attitudes, but the attitude of those in regular contact with the blind, that we should regard as important. The same may be said *vis-à-vis* the retarded. Among those in contact teachers are an important group. Efron and Efron (1967) found that special-class teachers expressed more favourable attitudes than teachers of ordinary children, whilst Gottlieb reports that only a minority of teachers favoured regular class placement. He notes with some concern that the movement for integrating the retarded child into the ordinary school is a strong one, but that 'regular education teachers do not possess special positive attitudes towards children labelled mentally retarded' (Gottlieb, 1975, p.120). He suggests that a move towards integration should be accompanied by programmes designed to influence and change teachers' attitudes.

The curious and sometimes contradictory results of research on attitudes to the retarded are partly due to variation in methods, and to samples being drawn from diverse backgrounds, but perhaps the gravest defect of much of the research is its failure to follow through the measurement of *expressed* attitudes into the field of actual person-to-person contacts.

The problems of attitude measurement have not been discussed here. The study of attitudes to handicaps falls into two broad types:

(1) Prevalence of specific attitudes towards handicaps.
(2) Relationship between attitudes towards disability and other variables (Yuker *et al.*, 1966, p.4).

Yuker lists the methods which have been used:

(a) Non-scored instruments—use of unstructured questionnaires.
(b) Variants of the above, using ranking techniques and socio-metric methods, the latter being especially prominent in work with children.
(c) Simple scored scales, involving either forced choices ('true-false', or 'agree-disagree') or five-point scales ('strongly agree', to 'strongly disagree').
(d) Attitude scales, using the appropriate psychometric methods.
(e) Other scorable tests.

He also comments that the bulk of research effort has been devoted to the attitudes of others towards disability and relatively few studies have focused on those of the disabled. Yuker notes that many of the attitude studies he reviewed contained weaknesses either because of over-simple methods, especially inadequate sampling, or of failure to tackle the questions of reliability. One of the most glaring faults in the research is not one of design or psychometric efficiency, but the way in which expressed attitudes are insidiously extrapolated to beliefs concerning public behaviour. Gottlieb points out that until a comparison is made between expressed attitudes and person-to-person behaviour, much of the value of paper-and-pencil attitude tests must remain uncertain.

4 Personality and self-image

The study of personality

In the previous chapter we suggested that the specific attitudes of those in close and regular contact with the handicapped were more significant than general social attitudes. The extent to which attitudes affect the direction of development of the handicapped person is clearly important. Is his personality influenced by the real constraints of disability, or the societal and personal attitudes to physical deviation, or some interaction between the two?

Personality is an elusive concept. There are almost as many definitions as there are views about its nature. The term obviously refers to qualities of the person, not to his moment-to-moment behaviour, but to some central aspects of his response to the social environment that are in some way representative. It is 'the more or less stable organization of a person's emotional, conative, intellectual, conceptual and physiological behaviour which determines to a large extent, his adjustment to environmental situations' (Griffiths, 1970, p.83). Personality is usually studied hierarchically; habitual behaviours are observed, and those which intercorrelate are seen as traits, while the intercorrelation of traits leads to the classification of types.

The study of the personality of handicapped children has considerable practical importance but unfortunately work on this aspect of their development has been somewhat sparse. Pringle

(1964) noted that there were few studies of the emotional development of blind children; Reed (1970) made a similar comment
about deaf children; Zigler (1966, p.145), writing on the retarded
child noted, with regret, that 'so little work had, emanating from a
personality point of view, been done with the retarded'; while
Pilling (1973) remarked on the lack of definitive studies of
adjustment and chronic illness.

One reason for the comparative neglect of personality studies is
the technical difficulty of assessing handicapped children. Conventional tests have to be modified for the blind; the deaf child finds it
hard to understand oral questions or instructions and to convey his
responses, as does one with a speech defect; the retarded child may
have only a limited awareness of the basis of his behaviour and a
restricted verbal ability for reporting or expressing his feelings.
Group paper-and-pencil tests are seldom appropriate, and the
demands of individuals testing plus the need for modifications
make the process of assessing the personality of the child a difficult
and laborious one. Specially designed tests area available, such as
braille versions of popular personality tests, but the standardization
problems are formidable. Wachs (1966) discusses the use of
projective and non-projective personality measures with the blind,
deaf, speech-handicapped, motor-disabled and the intellectually
retarded. In the former responses to questions are standardized,
while stimuli in the latter allow the subject to present his own
organization. The author also provides examples of the useful tests
and suggests others of possible value to the clinician.

The paucity of objective data has not prevented beliefs and
opinions emerging about the personality of the handicapped.
Social reality being a product of consensus, such beliefs are more
significant than what is known or not known. They operate to fill
the empirical vacuum.

There is a long history in philosophy and literature, as well as in
psychology, of concern with the relationship between psyche and
soma, so that it is hardly surprising that the handicapped should be
seen as a proving ground for speculation and study. The persistent
belief in the direct relationship between body and mind has been
nourished by superstition and popular sayings, by fiction and
biography. C.P. Snow (1968) could describe Rutherford, the
physicist, as having the 'soma of a great writer', and Hardy, the

mathematician, as having 'opaque brown eyes, bright as a bird's — a kind of eye not uncommon among those with a gift for conceptual thought'. Clinard (1968) cites several edxamples of how the academic mind has been fascinated with this issue, e.g. the relationship between height and type of crime committed (tall, thin men commit theft and tall, heavy men commit forgery), and one intriguing study — the relationship between red hair and banditry in the Wild West.

The attempts to link appearance and physique with behaviour identified with the work of Kretschmer (1926) and Sheldon (1942) have failed to show substantive evidence of a strong correlation even at the group level and certainly not at the individual level. 'In general, certain individual differences such as normal extremes of height and weight ... correlate weakly with behaviour characteristics ... These weak relativities become important in large populations' (Block, 1955, p.56). Despite this, however, there have been several attempts to show on theoretical grounds that extreme physical variations will influence personal development. We now turn to these theories (McDaniel, 1969), and their relative potentialities as explanatory devices (English, 1971).

Some theoretical positions

(a) *Individual psychology*   Among the propositions of Alfred Adler (1927) was that each individual personality is unique and develops in response to certain social impulses which include a sense of inferiority, the striving for superiority and intervening compensatory behaviour. The life-style of the person reflects a central Alderian theme of striving to overcome childhood feelings of being inferior to parents and to the world at large. Such feelings are not abnormal and are present in everyone. The disabled person has a special type of inferiority, 'organ inferiority', and thus an enhanced drive to establish his superiority. McDaniel notes that this concept of inferiority and its accompanying compensatory behaviour has been indiscriminately applied to the handicapped, though it can occur at the clinical level. Compensatory behaviour can be observed in many disabled persons (e.g. the increased selective attention of the blind to things heard) but this is different from a compensatory lifestyle. There is case evidence of them using their disabilities as instruments of social control, but this may derive from careful observation by them of the non-disabled using their appearance and physique for social control; it only becomes 'pathological' when practiced by those with a stigmatized physical deviation.

It is increasingly apparent that concepts of inferiority and compensation cannot cover the wide range of responses of disabled persons to their disability. At the clinical level these concepts may have some limited value but, as used in the rehabilitation literature, they are too restricting.

(b)   *Body image*   Attitudes to self and others are thought to be affected by perceptions of values attributed to appearance and physique. Persons place themselves on a continuum from those with a positively valued body image to those with a negatively valued one. For Schilder (1950) body image was closely identified with self-image. Body image is constructed from postural cues, tactile impressions, visual appearance, degree of functional effectiveness and from social reinforcement. The disabled person receives negative feedback from his own body and via the responses of others during his formative years, while his body image is being constructed. The negative reinforcement received by black children is made explicit when they draw and paint themselves as white. Richardson's work suggests that disabled children share the value system of non-handicapped peers, and we may assume that perception by the handicapped of the high value placed on normal physique provides a tension between actual and ideal body images. This tension is occasionally revealed in handicapped children's self-portraits where the area of physical deviation is either exaggerated or disregarded.

This view of personal or self-image is most valuable when there are marked abnormalities of physique or appearance. It may also be appropriate where chronic illness deprives the child of former physical skills or capacities, and this suggests its value for work on acquired disabilities.

(c)   *Somatopsychology*   This is the study of 'variations in physique that affect the psychological situation of a person by influencing the effectiveness of his body as a tool for action or by serving as a stimulus to himself or others' (McDaniel, 1969, p.11). Behaviour and physique are seen as interrelated and interactive. Thus, according to this position, the visibly disabled are given a subordinate social role and those with milder disabilities will suffer greater anxiety and frustration than the grossly handicapped, since the latter experience lower expectations or have more allowances made for them. This contradicts an often expressed view that poorer adjustment is associated with more severe handicap.

Three concepts derived from somatopsychology are valuable for understanding the emotional development of children: they are mourning, devaluation and spreading. Mourning, as applied to the disabled, refers to sadness and regret at the lack or loss of functional skills and seems similar to the feelings aroused by the death of someone close to us. During the mourning period the grieving person is preoccupied with recollections of the person who has died; rehabilitation workers have observed a similar response in the disabled. Mourning is not only a psychological state, it is a social obligation. There are certain 'requirements of mourning' associated with cultural or religious norms, and it must be appropriate to the degree of loss, and be followed by a period of readjustment and recovery. Loss of a limb or function may similarly depress a person, who is then expected to conduct himself appropriately for the degree of loss and to go through a period of readjustment. This is what is meant by 'coming to terms with the handicap' — at an individual level the period of mourning and its intensity of feelings will vary considerably, but it will not be expected to continue indefinitely.

Devaluation is the process by which the disabled person is seen as more handicapped than he actually is, while spreading refers to the self-perceptions of those who see their disability expanding from its original source to encompass the whole body or whole personality. Devaluation and spreading are closely related — indeed, the latter might be caused by the former.

As Wright (1960) pointed out, somatopsychology has failed to demonstrate a consistent relationship between personality and disability, but its subordinate concepts have great potential for gaining an understanding of the effects of disability on the individual.

(d) *Social role* Illness or disability is not only a physical phenomenon with accompanying psychological features, it prevents the person from performing a range of customary social roles. Health being the optimum condition for the performing of roles, illness grants a legitimate exemption from customary requirements which continues as long as the patient performs adequately in the new role — that of a 'sick' person. The 'sick role' involves presenting one's self for treatment, an acknowledgement that one is sick, a striving for recovery and active cooperation with those who are seeking to return one to optimum role capacity (Gordon, 1966).

Handicapped children can be seen as 'sick', for some of them are just that, whilst others may be considered as metaphorically sick and treated as if they really were so, though not all of them will be able to perform every aspect of the sick role, such as striving to get well or cooperating with healing agencies. Institutions in this context become locations for the chronically 'sick': the delinquent absconding from a community home is not striving to get well and the maladjusted child in a therapeutic community is expected to conform to the prevailing definition of illness there — e.g. when behaving in a disturbed way is seen as obligatory in the therapeutic process. Balbernie (1973, p.540) writes of 'becoming suspicious of the "good" unit, the place for delinquent or disturbed children where there is no delinquency or disturbance visible'. He is, of course, referring to those establishements where spontaneous behaviour is repressed by authoritarian control, but the social role expectation is explicit. One danger of perceiving handicapped children as sick is that like sick persons, they will have things done for them and to them and will largely be at the mercy of the professional healers and helpers, with the consequent loss of human dignity and independence.

Theories such as the ones described above, all appear to have some use in understanding the personal development of handicapped children. In order to gauge their relative power as explanatory tools, English (1971) examined the theories in the context of the behaviour of the disabled and the reactions of normals to disability, especially in connection with the effect of handicaps and early experiences, the psychological impact of disablement, the sociological aspects of prognosis for rehabilitation and attitude change. He developed twelve propositions (e.g. the stigmatization of the disabled can be reduced) and then considered which theories seemed to offer support for them. The theories he used were individual-psychology, psychoanalytic, body-image and social-role theories. Theoretical support, or lack of it, for a proposition was judged on a five-point scale.

English concluded that no single theory was sufficient to encompass our present knowledge of the psychological and sociological impact of handicap. In his view the effects of disability in childhood are best explained by reference to psychoanalytic theory and individual psychology; rehabilitation processes are best analysed with a combination of individual psychology and body-image theory, while sociological aspects are probably best derived from social-role theories. He found that the reactions of the disabled and of other people important to them could not be explained by any one theoretical stance, that there was a need for an eclectic approach to theoretical concepts, and that attempts to understand the personality of the handicapped offered a major challenge since a unifying theory was a necessary, but as yet distant, goal.

Personality and handicapped children

One of the continuous themes in the literature is the search for a distinctive pattern of personality associated with medical classification. Before considering some of the studies on the personality of handicapped children, we shall look at an example drawn from adults with tuberculosis, since the history of ideas concerning the 'tuberculosis personality' has many points of similarity to the study of the disabled child's personality.

Doctors noted that only a fraction of patients with the tubercle bacillus develop into clinical cases of tuberculosis. After eliminating the environmental factors that appear to precipitate the condition (malnutrition, fatigue, overcrowding), there appears to be a residue of psychological ones associated with it, such as stress within the family. From this there developed a belief in a distinctive 'tuberculosis personality', often described in contradictory terms — 'introverted, apprehensive, anxious, over-optimistic, depressed, strongly motivated sexually, childish, neurasthenic and mentally alert' (Garrett, 1953, pp.101-3). This changed to the view that even if different personality types contracted the illness, the toxins produced by it created the tuberculosis personality type. Later research showed clearly that there was no one distinctive personality type, but what emerged was that 'tuberculosis patients do show anxiety, mild neuroticism, discontent and depression, more often after than is found in the general population: but the same thing can be said for groups of patients hospitalized for various other chronic and even acute disease' (Garrett, 1953, p.103). The natural history of the 'tuberculosis personality' has parallels in others handicaps.

Foulke (1972) has shown how treating the personality of the blind as a unitary concept has led to much uncritical acceptance of the idea that there is a distinctive personality associated with blindness. To him, blindness is more properly regarded as a set of situational variables, and the personality itself is too complexly determined to be accounted for by a single variable such as loss of vision.

Similar views were once held about the 'epileptic personality'. What they have in common is a simplistic equating of soma and psyche — a one-to-one correspondence that satisfies some personal reactions to handicapped people. What is surprising is not that these views have been and are held, but that they have survived with such vigour. As with handicapped adults, attempts have been made to show that medically or clinically defined groups of children display the same types of behaviour and adjustment accounted for by a single situational variable — the handicap.

Personality and the visibly handicapped child Cerebral palsy usually results in children having a motor defect, though there are other secondary problems, e.g. of speech or perception. The motor defect is highly variable, which is one of the clinical characteristics of the group; in some cases it results in severely limited mobility, in others it is only apparent as regards delicate skills. Cerebral palsy affects 2.9 school-age children in every 1,000. There are three main types: spastic, with rigid muscles and exaggerated reflexes; athetoid, characterized by slow writhing movements; and ataxic, with its marked disturbance of balance.

Phelps (1948) developed a hypothesis that the type of cerebral palsy was directly related to personality type, the latter being caused by the child's physical status. The spastic's rigid muscles, he thought, led to the child becoming fearful of people and strange situations, while the athetoid's involuntary movements made him confident in novel situations. Block (1955) examined twenty spastic and eighteen athetoid children (medically classified) of near-average intelligence (IQ 96), who were eleven years of age. All of them had congenital or early acquired cerebral palsy; they were given projective tests, behaviour ratings were obtained, and detailed case histories prepared. Particular attention was paid to such aspects of the children's emotional life as interpersonal relationships, self-concepts, attitudes and adjustment to disability, and sublimation techniques. Phelp's view was examined through measures which focused on overt behaviour and on unconscious behavioural tendencies. The two groups were compared on all measures and 'analysis ... revealed no significant differences between the spastic and athetoid groups in emotional life, interpersonal relationships, self-concepts, attitudes towards disability and adjustment to disability ... It may be concluded with reasonable certainty that no psychological differences as defined and measured in this study exist between the cerebral palsied types' (Block, 1955, p.79).

Block, like others before and after him, did find that a number of disabled children were maladjusted, but the form of maladjustment was not dissimilar to that seen in non-handicapped children, and the causes of their problems were unknown. His study revealed the value of adding projective tests to the more customary behaviour ratings by adults, since these children appeared to suppress much of their emotional life. Projective tests revealed the extent of frustration and the reaction to frustration by ' ... aggression, withdrawal and fantasy compensations ... The presence of frequent feelings of depression, inferiority and intropunitive reaction suggests that guilt about being disabled is present' (p.80). Acceptance of the handicap by the child (as perceived by adults) would often mask unconscious rejecting attitudes to self, and since according to Gesell and Amatruda (1947) temperamental characteristics are the least affected by cerebral damage, perhaps we should look to the social experience of these children for a partial explanation of their disturbance. Clearly the most important finding is the absence of any direct link between physical type and personality. This historical byway may now seem to us a quaint if not faintly ludicrous example of an outmoded way of thinking about children, but it is valuable to be reminded that in comparatively recent times such views were held and held sufficiently strongly to need empirical refutation.

Another example involves children with visual handicaps. Langan (1970) comments on the longstanding interest in the relationship between personality and blindness. While there were clues in the autobiographies of blind persons, there was little systematic evidence, though the general view was that personality among the blind was as diverse as in the sighted community. The more empirical data hint that blindness tends to emphasize or over-exaggerate normal aspects of personality rather than to create specific types, and this is shown by a 'more active response to praise or blame, [while] frustration is experienced more quickly' (Langan, 1970, p.380). Langan concedes that within the diversity there appear to be, among blind children, three main subgroups: an active group enjoying movement and music; a passive one; and a 'motory' one with high drive, given to much jumping, clapping, skipping and shouting — these broad groupings reflect, not abnormal states, but exaggerated aspects of normal development.

Like Gottlieb, Langan believed that, regardless of community attitudes to blind adults, what matters where blind children are concerned is the attitudes and experiences provided by those in regular contact with them, though there is the ever-present danger of natural dependence leading to over-protection. Langan was not alone in being convinced that blind children react to their handicap mainly in terms of the attitudes of other people important to them. Lowenfeld (1974) states that most blind children grow up into emotionally stable adults, a point that Richardson (1968) makes when he states that the critical empirical question is why this is so. Lukoff (1972) suggests that blind people experience particular attitudes which tend to be positive (though these can be taken to extremes, e.g. when sympathy becomes over-solicitousness) and that although many blind people now reject this marked degree of over-protection it may yet be relatively easier to adopt an independent and individual stance as an adult following a childhood in which there has been much support and care. One might even claim that the radicalism of some blind persons only becomes possible when basic health, education and care needs have been satisfied. Somatopsychology suggests that partially-sighted children would find it more difficult to adjust than blind children, but the evidence is not clear on this point.

Communication difficulties   Reed (1970) noted that there were few studies of the emotional development of deaf children and contrasted these with the many examinations of their intellectual development. He quoted work suggesting that twice as many deaf children could be classified as emotionally disturbed or needing psychiatric help as members of a matched control group who could hear. Projective tests on pupils in a residential school revealed emotional under-development, delay in understanding inter-personal behaviour, and egocentricity. As to the problem of the personality assessment of deaf children, he thought it, at present, best ' ... accomplished through clinical observations and case histories than through formal testing although this approach ... needs an examiner with long experience of hearing-impaired children of all ages and different environmental conditions' (Reed, 1970, p.435). Myklebust (1964) found that among the deaf child's problems were distorted body image and a failure to internalize appropriate male or female roles. The somatopsychological view that the partially hearing may possibly have greater adjustment problems is countered by Bowyer and Gillies (1972), who dis-covered that there was little difference between the adjustment of deaf or partially hearing pupils on projective tests and teacher ratings, and that in general the type of maladjustment among the partially hearing was similar to that of an unselected school population. This was explained by the unsuspected compensatory mechanisms of deaf children, and the early identification combined with superior facilities that had been available to them.

   Goldberg, Lobb and Kroll (1975), in a study of 172 deaf children, found them to be psychiatrically a 'high risk' group for maladjustment, though they discovered no specific syndrome associated with deafness. Delay in becoming acquainted with interpersonal dynamics can be understood, given that such know-ledge is largely (though not entirely) mediated through language. We might expect that where deaf children appear retarded in language they would more quickly grasp the non-verbal aspects of interpersonal relationships.

Episodic disabilities: the case of epilepsy   It has been estimated that there are some 60,000 school-age children with epilepsy, only half of whom are known to the school health service (Henderson,

1974). Between 600 and 700 attended the six special schools for epileptic children. The electrical discharges associated with the overt symptoms may be general or localized in the brain, producing *grand mal*, with its loss of consciousness, violent jerking of the limbs and sometimes incontinence, or *petit mal* with its momentary loss of consciousness. Seizures can take place during the day or during sleep. The condition can respond to treatment — usually medication and a 'regular and temperate mode of living'. There has been widespread misunderstanding about its nature, such as beliefs that sufferers are 'possessed', are likely to go mad or become criminal. The anxiety provoked by epilepsy expressed itself in the past in prohibitions on marriage, segregation from the community and exclusion from much of ordinary social and economic life. Happily the worst features of earlier misconceptions have been reduced if not entirely eliminated (Hill, 1959).

A longstanding debate has centred on whether there is a distinctive personality associated with epilepsy, and on the extent and nature of behaviour disorders amongst epileptics. Bridge (1949) found that behaviour disorders were not due to the epilepsy but to a wide range of social and environmental forces. Pond (1952) believed that children with *petit mal* were either small, blue-eyed, fair-haired boys or rather darker, more untidy-looking girls, and that in personality they were stubborn, serious, passive, well-mannered but given to such neurotic symptoms as nightmares and severe anxiety. Among those with brain injury he found evidence of aggressive and of explosive, unpredictable behaviour. Halstead (1957) found epileptic children in a special school to have more behaviour disorders than non-epileptic children used as a control. Nuffield (1961) showed a relationship between behaviour disorders and neurological status. Children whose cause of epilepsy was located in the temporal lobe region of the brain showed a tendency towards aggression but were not particularly neurotic, while the reverse was true of the *petit mal* group. One of his conclusions was that environmental factors determine the presence or absence of behaviour disorders but that the nature of the latter is partly determined by the child's neurological status. Henderson (1974) states that between 12 and 20 per cent of epileptic children have serious behaviour disorders, the form of these being no different from that in other seriously disturbed children.

Tizard's (1962) discussion of the personality of epileptics is still valuable. She outlined the main theories supporting or denying the view that there is a common personality, or suggesting that epileptics are more neurotic, their personalities being similar to those of other organically damaged persons; and the claims that personality varies with the type of epilepsy. She concluded that while there were no grounds for the unique personality theory, other views had still to be evaluated because the existing studies could be criticized for weaknesses in method, such as failure to provide adequate controls and limited use of standardized personality ratings. Since this excellent review paper, the complex interaction of environmental and pathological factors have been studied.

Rutter, Graham and Yule (1970) took a representative sample of children with neuro-epileptic disorders, including 64 with un- complicated epilepsy. They found a high proportion to have psychiatric disorders (34.3 per cent) which was not accounted for by such variables as severity of handicap, visible marks or social factors such as prejudice and rejection, but was 'associated with the effects of dysfunction of the brain'. Factors which *were* associated included psycho-motor fits, socio-economic status (father's occupation), low IQ, reading retardation, and emotional disturbance in the mother.

> Psychiatric disorders in the child with a neuro-epileptic condition is multifactorially determined with neurological factors, intellectual and educational factors, socio-familial factors, all playing a part in causation. The child with organic brain dysfunction has a much greater susceptibility to psychiatric disorders than other children in the general population. (Rutter *et al.*, 1970, p.3)

Bagley's (1971) study was specifically designed to examine an interactional view of the personality and adjustment of epileptics and found, as other have, that they show a higher than usual incidence of psychiatric disorder — aggression, emotional behaviour and neuroticism, and anxiety. Using clinical data, interview schedules with parents and children and an index of brain injury, Bagley was able to show an association between psychiatric disorders and the index of brain injury, but in general his conclusion was that personality disturbance in epileptic children is related to the combination of several variables among which is epilepsy. Goldin and colleagues (1971) examined a somewhat older group (13-21), and showed clearly the impact of parental attitudes and family dynamics on the epileptic person's attitude to his schooling, vocational goals and interpersonal relationships, but again epilepsy was not directly implicated as a cause. If the type of disturbance in epileptics is similar to that in normals, it may be only at the interactional level of analysis that it can be understood.

Extrapolating from the evidence on emotional disturbance it seems reasonable to suppose that there exists among epileptics a range of personality not basically dissimilar from that of the general population, but more vulnerable. The evidence that epileptics are more disturbed (neurotic) is not strong — Rutter's study found the neuro-epileptic children significantly more 'worried and fussy' than other groups. The evidence that in personality epileptics are like other children with organic brain damage is not entirely unequivocal. Nor is the view that personality is related to type of epilepsy. But there is some evidence that seizures may be related to behaviour disorders, though the latter may in turn be related to the social stress associated with seizures.

None of the above studies have focused on what seems to be the central core of the epileptic's experience — loss of control over his body and the episodic nature of the handicap. Some attention has been paid to the stigma attached to epilepsy but relatively little has been written about its social-psychological basis in childhood except by Bagley. The search for personality patterns associated with epilepsy or its variants appears to be largely inconclusive — patterns of reactions and behaviour tend to be associated with a range of factors, and in the clustering of factors epilepsy is only one element.

Stigmatized conditions Severe mental handicap is one of the most stigmatized disabilities. Yet within this diverse group those with Down's syndrome (mongolism) have been described as happy and cheerful, fond of music, with a placid temperament. Blacketter-Simmonds (1953) found that DS children were as varied in personality as any other group of mental defectives of the same grade. More significantly Blacketter-Simmonds showed how investigators had progressively added to the list of positive traits. Silverstein (1964), using a more complicated rating system, compared DS children with others of the same age and sex, drawn from the same hospital ward. On Silverstein's scales DS children were rated significantly higher on traits such as general adjustment, cooperation, cheerfulness, etc. These findings seem to support popular beliefs but, as Silverstein notes, they were based on perceptions by workers who themselves might have been influenced by expectations of the children's personalities.

Jolly seems to accept the general view of DS children being friendly, placid and musical, but suggests that the characteristics do not derive directly from the condition but from parents' attitudes since 'the majority of parents of mongols, once given the facts, recognize that the child cannot do better, and do not pressurize him to achieve more than he is capable' (Jolly, 1971, p.17-18). The physical signs of mongolism are soon detected which mean that this pattern of parental attitudes is present from early childhood.

Nakauchi (1972) claims that characteristic traits *are* intrinsic to the syndrome and are not related to parental attitudes. In a study of 43 children with DS all living with their families, he eliminated all traits which were related to mental retardation in general and found that 'clownishness, musicality, marked mimicking ability, stubbornness, sociability, obedience, vividness and rambling chatter' were independent of age, sex, incidence of stigma, severity of retardation, or maternal attitudes. He did not find any evidence of a homogeneous set of attitudes among the mothers of his sample.

Belmont (1971) examined studies of the personality of DS children which had rigorously examined the stereotype, and found that many were based on a simple causal chain — chromosomal abnormality leading to stereotyped behaviour. There was a lack of appreciation of the long-term effects on the child of his interpersonal contacts and social environment, and of whether biological factors interact with particular socialization regimes to produce a 'specially hybridized' picture of adaptation which might be especially prominent in institutional settings. The simple medico-behavioural chain is unacceptable because children are never allowed just to develop; they grow within a web of interactions which influence the biological basis of behaviour, and many researchers had failed to allow for the effect of special environments.

The cumulative effect of Belmont's attack on the Down's syndrome stereotype is to collapse it — the longer lives of today's survivors allows us to see considerable variations in adult behaviour;

psychotic behaviour has been observed; and the study presents a (variable) picture of emotional disturbance in the group. Belmont considers that the balance of evidence seems to favour the view that DS children are somewhat less disturbed than other groups, but whether they have a pleasanter personality is dubious. What is unequivocal is that there is no uniform personality. Experimental evidence is against clinical impressions that they are musical, while claims that their social development is superior to their intellectual development are uncertain. The relationship between intelligence levels and clinical varieties of Down's syndrome has revealed little except the extent of the research difficulties involved in disentangling the problem.

The study of the personality of medically labelled groups appears to have gone through several stages. At the start there was usually an attempt to unveil the common personality characteristics on which stereotyped views were based. The second stage was often the breaking-down of the stereotype into patterns of behaviour and reaction associated with clinical sub-categories. Finally the view that the latter had common personality characteristics collapsed as the true extent of individual differences among children with a common handicap became apparent. It is difficult to explain why belief in a unilateral association between disability and personality persisted for so long even though clinical experience must have shown that the reverse was true. Quite slowly we have come to accept that the child's personality emerges from a complicated set of interchanges between his biological predispositions and the other people who are important to him, and neither are in any real sense uniform. It is most likely that from the almost infinite variety of attitudes and socialization practices and the range of handicapping conditions under any medical label, a uniform personality type would emerge. We are left, not with the comfort of stock expectations but the more difficult, though essentially more humane, task of reflecting on the children and their experiences as individuals.

If for the sake of argument we accept that children with certain types of disability display common behavioural characteristics, it would seem just as sensible to look for an explanation in their common socialization experiences as in their basic physical disabilities. Regularities in behaviour might just as easily be the result of being treated, taught or institutionalized in a more or less uniform manner. Paradoxically, as treatment and socialization of the handicapped has moved away from regimentation to a more personal approach (revealing *en route* the variety of individual responses to handicaps), we may begin to see more clearly than ever before, the real relationships between psyche and soma — or the question may finally be relegated to the scrapheap of psychological speculation.

If personality studies have been unable to find a perspective for this problem, where should we look for an overview? Some writers have found it unrewarding to approach the handicapped child's behaviour through the primary medical categories of conditions, and have discovered a more fruitful frame of reference in role theory, which is not anchored to specific medical labels.

Role theory

Role theory has been most consistently applied to handicapped children in the case of those who are chronically ill.

The person who becomes ill has to deal with a new role, that of the sick person, with its inbuilt tension between past and present. Each person occupies a variety of social positions — father, teacher, son, etc. — and with each position is associated a set of 'social norms, demands, rules and expectations that specify the behaviours that an occupant of that position may appropriately initiate towards an occupant of some other position ... role is defined as the set of prescriptions defining the behaviour of an occupant of one position towards other related positions' (Johnson, 1970, p.44). In the 'sick' role the 'prescriptions' involve an exemption from some of the responsibilities associated with position; but there must be shown a desire to get well and to cooperate with those attempting to heal.

Gordon (1966) suggested three significant role relationships: doctor-patient; family-patient; and self(ego)-patient. Each could be examined in terms of four possible reactions to illness: dependence (a tendency to give up some areas of responsibility whilst retaining a residue of independence); normal independence (retaining the responsibilities inherent in the status 'well'); over-independence (demanding more independence when sick than when well); and self-pity (rejecting the possibilities of self-help). There are many implications here for the study of the development of children: for example, is there a correlation between one two-sided relationship and another? Is the patient-physician role modified when the patient is a child? What are the long-term consequences for personality development of a child being chronically sick? To be obliged to take a particular role (almost irrespective of the physiological cause of the handicapping condition) may produce similar patterns of behavioural reaction.

Fishler and colleagues (1972) studied a group of 45 children with a rare condition, galactosemia, requiring a special diet. (Galactosemia is a hereditary fault in carbohydrate metabolism and produces such symptoms as vomiting, failure to thrive, loss of weight, cataracts and jaundice.) The researchers followed this group from early childhood to adulthood, using various tests, appropriate to the state of development, such as draw-a-person, sentence completion, Rorschach (ink-blot test) and TAT (the Thematic Apperception Test in which the subject describes what he sees in a series of illustrations which are open to a variety of interpretations and hence are thought to tap unconscious feelings and attitudes). Their results showed that there were definite changes according to age. The pre-school child was seen as 'excessively shy and fearful in terms of personal contacts'. During the school-age period there were many signs of anxiety, such as nail-biting, and at adolescence there were a few children with very serious problems of adjustment. There was 'little doubt that their poor self-image was related to their dietary restrictions which clearly set them apart from other persons. These feelings of inadequacy were further compounded by learning problems at school' (Fishler *et al.*, 1972, p.416).

Olch (1971) investigated 45 children and young adults with haemophilia, a condition characterized by recurrent haemorrhages which may be spontaneous or caused by (even minor) injury. Prolonged hospitalization or intensive care is usual. Olch gave her subjects draw-a-person and Rorschach ink-blot tests and need-achievement measures. In the 5-7 age group she found a common anxiety, intense feelings of inadequacy and social unease. The 8-12 age group were passive, lacked spontaneity and were keenly aware of the difference between themselves and others. The young adolescents showed the greatest activity, resistance and independence, while the older ones 'exhibited the greatest constriction of personality. They relied heavily upon intellectualization, compulsivity and avoidance of spontaneity.'

These two studies are particularly interesting since they cover the child's developmental period. They both give some support to somatopsychological theories and to role theory. Olch suggests that in haemophilia patients, limited activity produces a restricted thought process. Neither produces any evidence for a distinctive personality type, but both indicate a pattern of adaptation to prescribed roles.

Similarly, asthma, the psychosomatic condition *par excellence*, has failed to reveal a special personality type, though Pinkerton and Weaver (1970) noted the similarity of their asthmatic patients to other sick children. Anxiety, dependency and neuroticism influenced the asthmatic child's immediate interpersonal milieu. Other studies have found low levels of reactivity, tension and depression in asthmatic children, highly reminiscent of Olch's observations of haemophiliacs. Swift, Seidman and Stein (1967) found that children with diabetes had a poor self-image and showed dependence, anxiety, oral preoccupations and depression.

Broadly speaking, these studies of such children, whether suffering from physical or psychosomatic conditions, show a degree of adaptive response which cannot solely be explained by their illness. What gives the developing picture some coherence is that the adaptive pattern emerges from role expectation. The experience of limited everyday activities and the anxiety caused by illness and its treatment appear to produce, in Gordon's terms, a role behaviour consonant with dependence and self-pity. The particular value of the Fishler and Olch studies is that they show the role not to be constant over the developmental period. In the early period there is unsettledness, giving way to passivity in the latency period, challenged by resistance and independence in pre-adolescence and followed by rigidity and compulsion later on. However, while these studies lend weight to the sick role theory, we should be cautious about accepting the findings too uncritically, for there are still some unresolved questions about the sample sizes used, the particular environments in which the children developed and the under-use of other possible explanatory variables such as parental attitudes.

An extension of this view of the significance of role is to be found in the work of Minde and colleagues (1972), who examined the psycho-social development of a group of physically handicapped children. The youngest children appeared to regard themselves as non-handicapped, but as having a functional disability. This they saw as extraneous to them — an inconvenient encumbrance — and in time the functional loss would be made good. This response underwent a significant change when they were placed in a residential school for the physically handicapped. At first, many children went through a period of profound melancholy due to two factors — separation from home and the realization that miraculous cures were unlikely. Children could see other, older children, with similar disabilities. Eventually, though it could take a long time, they came through this depressed phase, and the transformation was marked by statements they made about their future which showed a view of the self that included their disablement. Minde comments on the gradual and sometimes painful process by which these children made the transition from one status to another.

Self-image

How a person perceives and appraises himself can be described and interpreted in a number of ways. Self-appraisal or self-concept has a developmental component which in the child refers to the extent and manner in which innate predispositions, biological growth and maturation affect his view of himself. It also has a social component — a view of self derived from interactions with others, especially those who are important to the child. Self-concept develops out of the organism's interaction with the environment and the value systems of others, and out of the need to have a consistent view of the self, and is subject to modification through learning. Argyle (1973) provides an economical view of self-concept as consisting of self-image, i.e., how the person sees himself, and self-esteem — the value he places on himself.

Both self-image and self-esteem will be influenced by perceptions of the attitudes of others, especially of those whose opinion is most prized. Thomas (1971) showed that among ten-year-olds the influence of the family on the formation of self-concepts was more significant than that of peer groups, though we would expect changes here with the approach of adolescence. Children acquire a generalized view of the qualities, abilities and skills that command social approval, and compare their own attributes with those that are approved. Here some discrepancy may intrude between an actual and a desired or ideal self-image, and self-concept research implies that for sound mental health this discrepancy should not be too great.

Measures of self-concept are usually either observational or of the self-report variety. I. Gordon (1966) has shown the value of observational methods with retarded subjects who could not complete a self-report, but of course they are not free from bias in behaviour sampling or interpretation. Wylie (1961) notes that self-report devices can be inaccurate or misleading, since the subject may deicde to present a view of himself that is partial or socially desirable, or he may interpret items in a highly personal way. Increasing dissatisfaction with self-report has led some writers to recommend repertory grid methods as having fewer disadvantages (Kelly, 1955; Nash, 1973). In its original form, the repertory grid test asked the subject to consider twenty people in groups of three at a time, and to state how two of them differed from the third. The responses express ways of classifying people and are termed 'constructs'. The method's main attraction is that the constructs are provided by the subject himself, and not predetermined by the tester. Most studies of handicapped children, however, have used self-report measures; two groups in particular have been studied — the retarded and the physically handicapped.

Because of the technical problems of the validity and reliability of self-concept measures when used with retarded children, we must agree with Lawrence and Winschel (1973) that many of the findings are at best inconclusive. Self-concept measures of retarded children have been correlated with age, sex, social class, intelligence, length of special schooling, and presence in special classes or integrated settings. The findings are often contradictory as well. At face value they suggest a modest correlation with intelligence, that retarded girls have a higher self-concept than retarded boys, and that high levels of self-esteem are given by educationally subnormal boys in a special school compared to those in secondary schools. But the research picture on the whole is confused.

The studies of physically handicapped children appear to be more consistent. Garlinghouse and Sharp (1968) examined the relationship between self-concept, family stress and the number of 'bleeding episodes' experienced by a group of 18 haemophiliac children aged between 9 and 14. The children were placed in front of a chart containing 36 profile silhouettes diminishing in height from left to right. Using a pointer each child indicated the place he would occupy on the chart according to his height and thirteen other dimensions. Family stress was estimated via a questionnaire for mothers, and records of bleeding episodes were obtained. There was a moderately strong relationship between high self-concepts and fewer episodes of bleeding, but stress was directly related to frequency of bleeding, irrespective of the level of self-concept. It was thought that self-concepts acted as mediators between the children's physical status and their perceptions of stress.

Nussbaum (1962) studied a group of adolescents with cerebral palsy in order to determine their self-concepts, and the concepts held of them by their mothers, about capacity to perform tasks, social relationships, vocational potential and intelligence. He discovered significant correlations between the adolescents' own self-concepts and their mothers' concepts of them in three of the areas — tasks, social relationships and vocational potential — and he concluded that the mothers appeared to influence the self-concepts of their children.

Smits (1964) studied the influence of the obviousness and severity of disability on adolescents' self-concepts, using a self-concept and self-acceptance measure. Those with mild disabilities had higher self-concept scores than those with severe ones; severely disabled girls had the lowest self-acceptance scores, and the more obviously disabled adolescents received more extreme ratings from classmates than did the others.

Kinn (1964) examined differences in the self-reports of 72 physically handicapped and non-handicapped children, as well as discrepancies between actual and ideal self. The handicaps included sensory, orthopaedic, circulatory and metabolic disorders. As might be expected, the handicapped children saw themselves as less physically adequate than the non-handicapped; they had fewer close relationships and fewer opportunities for social participation, and though they had similar life-goals to the non-handicapped, they felt less able to achieve them. The visibly handicapped showed greater correspondence between self-concept and ideal self than did the non-handicapped.

Grinter (1974) studied the self-concepts and ideal selves of visually handicapped adolescents, and found that they did not have a lower self-concept score than did a control group. They did, however, show a greater discrepancy between perceived and ideal self, and there was an association between low self-concept scores and ratings of social adjustment. (A useful discussion of self-concept in handicapped children may be found in Shakespeare's *The Psychology of Handicap*, 1975.)

Self-concept studies are ones to which many students are attracted, partly because of the intrinsic interest of the topic and partly because of the simplicity in the completion and scoring of self-concept measures. However, a cautionary note must be sounded both with respect to the uncritical use of potentially unreliable instruments, and to the interpretation of findings without adequate checks such as the use of social desirability scales.

5 The socialization of the handicapped child

Socialization processes

Children are born with biological systems that allow behaviour to be patterned by and adapted to their social surroundings. Those persons with strategic positions in the child's world are more than caretakers, since they mediate between him and the prevailing social order, and through them he starts the process not only of learning about that social order, but also his place within it. Socialization can be broadly defined as ' ... the inculcation of the skills and attitudes for the playing of given social roles' (Mayer, 1970, p.xii). The young child learning these skills and attitudes is sometimes seen as almost totally plastic when faced with cultural pressures to acquire 'given social roles' — thus, his personality will be what his culture demands. This extreme view is untenable since the individual is not totally plastic or passive in acquiring social roles, nor does he develop in a society which demands rigid conformity to cultural pressures; moreover, even if there were wide agreement about the most desirable outcome of socialization (and there is not), the process is not in the hands of people able to give the necessary amount of conditioning. All this suggests that in our society the outcome is dubious rather than assured.

We can observe societies where there appears to be almost universal (public) agreement about the social roles required of the adult and about the ways of inculcating the skills and values associated with them. Loudon (1970), in his work on teasing and socialization on the remote island of Tristan de Cunha, noted the widespread agreement, in a small and vulnerable community, about the value to adults of avoiding open displays of aggressive feelings — the avoidance of such displays was a significant part of the social training of their young children. Comparisons between our own apparently more varied and implicit socialization programmes and those of other societies where there is a greater consensus on practice and outcomes readily come to mind (Bronfenbrenner, 1974).

One of the purposes of the planned inculcation of social roles is the promotion of social stability. This is a mechanism of social continuity, and the more accurately a society can identify these roles, the more effectively it can teach the associated values and attitudes, and so correspondingly protect itself from the tension of change and uncertainty. Much of children's experience can properly be regarded as anticipatory role-playing, and throughout childhood they progressively acquire the behaviours which will most contribute to a socially cohesive adult role; being anticipatory it also allows for failure and inadequcies to be corrected.

The internalization of role behaviour appear to involve two major aspects of learning — imitation and identification. Imitation is the modelling of behaviour on that of an admired other person. Modelling leads not to the absorption of specific habits but to global patterns of action, and the strength of the desire to imitate is related to the model's status and position and the quality of the emotional relationship between model and imitator. When he identifies with the model, the learner makes either a conscious or unconscious attempt to become that other person. As with imitation the model's status and the quality of relationship affects the success or otherwise of the process. If the model is both powerful and enjoys a warm close relationship with the learner, identification is more probable.

Not all social learning is embraced by imitation or identification. Some aspects are acquired from a concern for general social approval, and this appears to be more marked in the area of learning specific habits, but the major significance of imitation and identification lies in the combined effect the model has both as a person and as a role-exemplar since he is often not simply himself but a whole social category.

With us, socialization is not often the complete responsibility of any single agency. For the vast majority of children the process relies on several, and they, in sequence, take up a distinctive and even superordinate position. The main agencies are family, schools, peer groups, religious bodies and occupational groups. The family is still the primary one and continues its responsibilities to the child for as long as he remains a member; not only is it the first, but it is often thought to be the most significant agent. The personality of the child is fashioned within the family, and there he learns his first and crucial lessons about the roles which society will expect from him. The family is a special type of social system in which there is a paradox: the young child can invest all his emotional resources in it, yet eventually he must become emancipated from it, and the management of this dependence-independence function is probably one of the most difficult tasks of this specialized social system.

Some anthropologists refer to the whole socialization process within a culture as a 'vernacular system'. This includes all those practices for which explicit results are claimed. The theories, rituals, ceremonies, techniques, rewards and punishments collectively comprise the vernacular system — the conscious, deliberate attempts to mould the young into patterns of behaviour consistent with the society's values and attitudes. It can be objected that our own practices consist of not one, but several sub-systems. Given a society in which the adults do not appear to underwrite a consensual or uniform prescription we are dealing with diversity rather than homogeneity. Our vernacular systems vary greatly over time — witness the changes in views about children and their development from Victorian England to the present day — variations of a social nature, as illustrated by the different socialization practices of different social classes so vividly documented by Klein (1965), and regional variations which still seem to exist, for example, in the different attitudes and practices towards physical punishment in Scotland and in England. Admittedly there are pressures towards greater uniformity, but at the present time variability rather than consensus looks to be a more accurate reflection of socialization practice.

One consequence of social and economic mobility in an industrial society has been to throw into sharper relief the central role of the family in the socialization process. A characteristic of the present family (and it is still alive and well) is that it is a small social system which brings about a greater degree of reciprocal dependence between adult members than in earlier times. The erosion of the extended kin network and the parallel encroachment of specialized agencies such as schools, social services and peer groups, means that the small family has additional responsibilities for socializing its young members. The marriage relationship becomes more strategic since, as Parsons (1951) puts it, mobility may leave the family effectively kinless and the marital partnership structurally unsupported. Largely from its own psychological resources, the small family has to provide those skills, experiences and models which formerly could be enriched by a network of relatives or by a cohesive community. Perhaps what is central here is that the parents are increasingly crucial, since the mother and the father are significant models for sex-role differentiation.

Mobility and social fragmentation also imply that the parents, who perform the primary acts of socialization, and do so without the checks and balances inherent in most extended social systems, are tending to seek support and rationale for their activities by reference to outside experts — part of the process known as the professionalization of parenthood. This leads to presenting parenthood as both a moral and technical responsibility which extends from the details of feeding and toilet-training to more global aspects of behaviour and attitudes. For instance, Spock's famous *Baby and Child Care*, which began as a medical aid for parents who did not have easy access to doctors, has become a handbook of socialization practice. He writes of parents' responsibilities to bring up children with a greater respect for law and order and other peoples' sensibilities: ' ... there are many ways in which we could and should teach them these attitudes' (Spock, 1968, p.284); this indicates a significant shift away from a permissive child-centred approach to one which suggests an explicit socialization outcome.

The socialization process is one of becoming human in the way in which 'human' is defined by particular agents and particular cultures, but what appears to be distinctive about our own socialization practices is an absence of agreed objectives. Of course, we might argue that at least one agreed objective is not to have one. Given that society is changing quite rapidly, the inculcation of skills for given social roles has to be replaced by skills of engagement in roles as yet only dimly perceived, and socialization becomes the task of adapting the new roles — in effect, a process of socialization for socialization.

Disability and socialization

The existence of disability in children may mean that the process and outcome of socialization differ in some respects from those experienced by non-handicapped children. Attitudes towards disability or handicap, and differences according to types or severity, would appear to be factors affecting the socialization process. Given the variations in socialization practices, it seems unlikely that even if there were differences between the socialization experiences of the handicapped and non-handicapped the differences themselves would be uniform.

One way in which socialization practices will be influenced is through the *direct* effects of the disability itself — the sorts of limitation or hindrance imposed by it on the use of the full range of customary social learning methods. This is most obvious in the case of children with profound sensory disabilities. Deafness in an infant prevents his mother from using words as means of outside control; he is slow to acquire an internal language by which to regulate his own behaviour (in the manner which Luria (1963) suggests occurs with normal children); he is also slow to acquire social concepts which are heavily dependent upon language (see Kates and Kates, 1965): all these factors imply that the mechanism of social role learning will be directly affected by the handicap. Visually handicapped children will not receive that rich source of information, non-verbal signals, which parents customarily use in monitoring and controlling their children's behaviour. Children with severe physical handicaps may be effectively cut off from the crucial adjustive experiences of the peer group, unless very special efforts are made to provide these experiences. The direct effects of disabilities that present additional problems for parents or other caretakers do not, of themselves, imply that the outcomes are necessarily atypical, for the child can develop into a conventional social being even if exceptional measures are required.

Where parents see that their child and his disability are likely to meet rejection or indifference, the socialization process can be constrained. Perceptions of public attitudes may lead parents to restrict the social learning programme they prefer. Such *indirect* effects can be seen in the case of children with severe facial deformities. The French surgeon, Tessier, who has specialized in the remodelling of facial abnormalities is convinced of the value of early cosmetic treatment ' ... before irretrievable personality damage is done ... one must never forget that most of these patients are considered as monsters and as such are hidden by their families or shunted into institutions by society which often equates this physical deformation with mental subnormalities' (Sereny, 1972, p.21). Such concealment is based on a fierce desire to prevent the child from being hurt, the family forming, as Goffman puts it, a 'protective capsule' for its young. 'Self-belittling definitions of him are prevented from entering the charmed circle' (Goffman, 1968, p.46). We can see the same sort of thing in the impressive surgical work which is now carried out on infants with cleft palates and hare-lips and which dramatically minimizes the social effects of the conditions. Not all handicaps produce such constraints on social learning but these indirect factors, where they exist, are often more significant than direct ones. Direct and indirect effects can, of course, coexist in a family's responses to its handicapped child.

One of the results of severe handicap is that the natural time-scale within which the family and other socialization agencies undertake their respective tasks has to be modified. The clearest example is the mentally handicapped child: he reaches developmental milestones very slowly, and his extended period of learning means for the parents a continuing role in socialization well beyond that performed with their non-handicapped children. With normal children we find a harmony in the mental and physical duet where age, physical growth, and mental and social development proceed in regular though changing articulation and interaction. The retarded child shows a discrepancy between physical and social learning skills, and if retardation may be described as an everlasting childhood it is paralleled by an everlasting parenthood. Similarly, the grossly disabled child — e.g. one with muscular dystrophy — may progressively reverse the sequence of social learning as his deteriorating condition requires care of the kind usually given to infants. A limited and incomplete socialization programme is one of the clearest differences between the handicapped and the non-handicapped, although this only applies to those with the gravest disabilities since there are many others who are able to sustain a conventional adult role.

Thus, in short, the combination of direct and indirect effects and the extended time-scale place an added responsibility on the family. Just as we noted the increasing pressures on families with normal children, so we also find that no matter how sophisticated and elaborate the supportive services of medicine, education, welfare agencies and voluntary societies, the handicapped child's family will be called upon to provide the daily supervision and guidance of his social experiences. From the details of basic care to the provision of effective role models, it will need to make greater efforts over an extended period to achieve comparable results, and in some cases this additional responsibility has to be continuous and permanent.

One particular aspect of social learning may be greatly affected by the intensified parent-child contacts that come about when a child is a disabled one, and that is the learning of appropriate sex roles. Two problems arise here. The first stems from the tendency to deny the disabled a conventional sex role; it seems as though society is only slowly awakening to the sexuality of the disabled, and in the past there was an implicit denial of it and its role-associated behaviour. The second problem derives from the role models provided by parents, as when the father, being involved in giving care, emphasizes the more expressive (feminine) aspects of his paternal role and, relatively speaking, underplays the instrumental (masculine) side of his role.

Like all parents, those with handicapped children are likely to find their natural skills as parents supplemented by professional advice. Indeed they are at the extreme end of the 'professional-ization of parenthood' dimension since they are often given, and seek, the advice of doctors, psychologists and experts from the voluntary societies. Those who take such advice find that it usually involves direct technical assistance as well as more global counsel-ling about the long-term objectives of parenthood. It appears to be of at least three types. Firstly, there is the advice which contains nothing new but would not have been given unless the parents had a handicapped child. For example, a pamphlet for parents of visually handicapped babies states that ' ... parents must, therefore put aside some time each day to play with their child'. The second type of advice again consists of little that is unusual, but does underline or intensify common practice — for example, parents of a deaf child are counselled to ensure that he is 'doing things as often as possible: experimenting, pushing, pulling, watching, learning, etc.... rarely sitting idle without something interesting or stimulating in front of [him] ... making the most of the way in which the child spends his time means that parents must think really hard about it.' The third kind of advice is usually technical, being related to specific methods of treatment or rehabilitation. In a few cases this is so radical that it demands a new programme — the most extreme example is the Doman-Delacato system of patterning exercises for brain-injured children: ' ... each [child] is given a sequence of activities to perform usually lasting 15 minutes, and this sequence is repeated anything from 10 to 18 times a day every day of the year' (Wilkes, 1972, p.37). The technical aspects are not usually so demanding.

In recent years there has been a change in the upbringing of severely handicapped children and it is no longer seen as desirable for them to be separated from their parents at a very early age, as used to happen with blind children. Increasingly parents are seen as capable and responsible persons who with support and advice are competent, even superior socializers.

It is perhaps somewhat curious to speculate whether such advice, however clearly well-intended, is useful or not for the families involved. Coming from authoritative sources it probably provides much-needed support for parents either by reinforcing existing practices or introducing them to more effective ones. Clearly if the trend of the advice fits in with prevailing values and attitudes, new strategies will not cause psychological stress. Where the advice involves a profound shift in attitudes, again this can be accommodated if it results in demonstrable improvements in the child's behaviour or learning. However, where demonstrable improvements are not achieved in spite of authoritative advice, there is a tendency to believe that the fault does not lie in the advice but in the parents. Those offering advice should guard against creating such an opportunity for parents to feel inadequate.

The subculture of handicap

Before looking at specific examples of socialization, it may be opportune to examine handicap as a subcultural phenomenon. Goodman (1972) described childhood itself as a culture which ' ... like all cultures is learned, shared and transmitted. It is in some degree learned by children from one another. Mainly it is learned from adults. It is learned but not necessarily taught.' We catch the flavour of what Goodman means by the culture of childhood in the particular language of that culture as depicted by the Opies (1959). All children develop in 'a series of interlocking cultural contexts, all of them changing in some degree, some in harmony, some in conflict ... ' (Blyth, 1968, p.39). Blyth suggests that these 'cultural contexts' include nationality, rural or urban setting, social class, neighbourhood, sex-role divisions, peer group, the common experience of schooling and the specific culture of the child's family. Each context has its roles, rules, norms and other ingredients such as language, attitudes and values. Collectively they comprise a set of distinctive but not isolated experiences, each one at various times assuming a degree of primacy. The significance of these contexts is that they involve groups, the members of which are mostly of around the same age. As a result, individuals acquire the values, attitudes, language and images of the group, and the totality of shared experiences provides the basis of *belonging* — in the sense used by Bettelheim (1971) of having a rightful place — the foundation for identity formation and secure membership of the social order.

Some handicapped children are not able to participate fully in these cultural contexts. Their cultural experiences differ from those of others in their age group because of prolonged periods in hospital, separate forms of schooling, institutionalization, restriction on mobility or over-protection. One aspect of this anomalous social experience is the handicap itself. Each category becomes a specific socialization experience.

> Society talks of 'the blind', 'spastic', 'the maladjusted', 'gifted children' and so forth, and reinforces this classification with institutional provision for each, so that it ... is likely that the children must classify themselves accordingly, taking others who share

their abnormality as one of their major reference groups. (Blyth, 1968, p.40)

If successful socialization partly depends on a body of shared experiences, then an individual who fails to acquire such a common stock will find it more difficult to secure a rightful place in his culture. The more distinctive the 'culture of handicap', the more difficult the integration into the larger community. The more successfully the handicapped person adjusts to the culture of handicap, the harder will be his task of participating in the full range of conventional social roles. Among the distinguishing features of the culture of handicap are: exposure to extreme attitudes — either over-protection or rejection; involuntary association with others similarly handicapped; frequency of hospitalization; special education; lifelong bureaucratic structures — sheltered workshops, colonies, total institutions; restrictions on the full range of adult roles; and awkwardness in social interaction. In some cases these may be summarized as resulting in a subordinate social status and a role of dependence.

Before examining one of the agents of socialization — namely the school — we shall look at the socialization of particular groups of children.

The socialization of handicapped children: some examples

Much of the research on the socialization of blind children has focused on differences between them and sighted children, and one surprising conclusion is that most intelligent blind children find a valid role for themselves in adult society. Given the nature of their handicap, their socialization appears to be remarkably successful. Scott (1969) suggests that this success presents many difficulties for those who tend to see disability as automatically equated with deviant social status. The problems confronting the blind with additional handicaps is another matter as Myers (1975) makes clear. Most blind children with no other disability appear to acquire the social skills for successful community membership. Scott argues that three features of their social development — language and experience, self-image and social roles — deserve special attention.

The blind child perceives the world through sound and through what he can touch, manipulate or reach — an environment largely made up of stationary objects and of events within his hearing range or mediated through language. Sight is our dominant sense, and our language reflects this. The blind infant's schematic apprehension of objects by touch alone is a perceptual process which differs from that of the sighted child, although both may come to identify the object by a common verbal label. Often, differences in apprehension are relatively unimportant but when the 'object' is another person, a complex social situation or an abstraction, the differences in the sensory basis on which concepts are constructed may be significant. The acquiring of language without having crucial visual feedback has led to the charge that some of the verbal facility of the blind is empty of content. This can occur, but the vital point seems to be missed — namely that language is the key to becoming human. After Washoe, the ape who mastered a complex sign language, we cannot claim that language distinguishes man from the animals, but it is the most important social attribute for full membership of our culture and it is an undamaged skill for most blind children. Their language ability is the essential mechanism for social acceptance. Through special aids such as braille books and typewriters, the blind have access to the literature of their society; they can communicate their response to this heritage, and only the visual arts are beyond them.

Absence of visual feedback is thought to affect self-image since this absence, coupled with the less strong external stimuli that result from the external environment being limited to what is within reach or hearing, enhances what is ever-present — the self. The centrality of the self — preoccupation with the body and personal feelings and ideas — apparently leads to an extended period of egocentricity. Deep interest in the self results in a limited capacity to view events and social relationships from the perspectives of others.

Perhaps the most significant impact of blindness is on role-learning and role-taking. In this area of social learning, visual scanning and imitation are important for sighted children; the visually handicapped have to learn from linguistic cues. Young blind children may have limited opportunities for the reciprocal role-taking that occurs during play and interaction with peers. If the limitation inherent in the disability is compounded by over-protective attitudes, they will be further restricted in experimenting with roles. They are incapable of perceiving the non-verbal signals which accompany speech and social behaviour, and have difficulty in acquiring these as part of their own repertoire of social skills. Many writers have noted the 'silent faces of the blind' — a lack of facial expressiveness which seems to place some obstacles in the way of effective communication. Not only is the range of expressive accompaniments of speech reduced, but a minority of blind children are prone to mannerisms, such as eye-rubbing and rocking, which are interpreted by the sighted community as evidence of peculiarity or social inadequacy which further constrains social interactions. Though we have attempted to explain the successful adjustment of blind persons as the result of their intact language, part of the explanation must also be community attitudes to blindness. These, albeit containing elements of pity and patronage, have been positive attitudes translated into services and institutions which in turn, however, have developed a generation of blind people now deeply critical of these very attitudes and resources.

Physical handicap, particularly in those forms which seriously restrict mobility, is a variable limitation which prevents or inhibits the acquiring of developmental skills at the appropriate ages. Like blind children, the physically handicapped grow up in a restricted environment, although it is richer by its visual dimension. Exploration of that environment is not easy and while the youngster may find his curiosity impeded by his disablement, he has the chance to observe and imitate the social behaviour of others. Again like blind children, physically handicapped children, given that they may be more isolated and have prolonged hospital treatment, may develop a preoccupation with self. They may have a marginal status, it being uncertain whether they are members of the world of the normal child or that of the permanently disabled, and spending their formative years with others similarly incapacitated may encourage them to see the disabled as their primary social reference. Protective institutions dealing only with disabled children have the advantage of providing a sympathetic environment in which confidence can be built up, and the disadvantage of shielding them from the full extent of the problem they are likely to meet outside its comforting embrace.

The physically handicapped are such a varied group that to generalize about their socialization is unlikely to take us very far. Those with multiple problems — speech, hearing, perceptual and cognitive difficulties — on top of the primary physical handicap, present quite different challenges from those with minor disabilities, intact sensory systems and normal speech. Those with declining physical powers — as in muscular dystrophy — provide totally different problems to socializers from those whose conditions are stabilized or responding positively to treatment.

However, there does seem to be one overriding issue and that is the issue of dependence. In varying degrees disabled children are dependent on others. All young children are dependent on adults, but their development is one of accelerating independence. The unfolding of skills and abilities changes the person from someone who cannot do things to one who increasingly can. Disability may imply an unchanging dependence on adults in many areas of personal life. The task for socializers is to confine their care strictly to the disability while maximizing the child's independence in every other way. It is all too easy for concern to envelop the child in such a protective blanket that unavoidable dependence generates a totally dependent attitude.

Retarded children are another problem entirely. In the past, differences between their performance and that of normal children in learning tasks, were attributed to differences in cognitive ability. Since the mid-1960s there has been a re-examination of these differences and it now seems that a proportion of them must arise from non-cognitive factors, such as anxiety, stress and fear of failure. Increasingly it is recognized that failure in social adjustment in the retarded, is more closely related to personality variables such as low self-evaluation, over-dependence and anxiety. The presence of these variables is best explained by reference to 'atypical social histories', as Zigler (1966, p.146) has it. Among the features which can contribute to the latter are separation, cultural deprivation, and institutionalization; these result in higher anxiety levels, dependence (a heightened desire to interact with supportive adults) and its reverse (avoidance of adult interactions), and a pervasive expectancy of failure that leads to avoiding it rather than to seeking success.

The search for causal explanations of deficiencies in learning or social adjustment led in the past to an under-estimation of the extent to which the retarded person's social experiences contribute to his cognitive, emotional and interpersonal development. Many of the so-called characteristics of retarded children cited as typical of the clinical picture, are in fact products of socialization. Proof of the changes that can occur when people are taken away from institutions to more stimulating environments shows how closely the behaviour even of retarded persons is a function of social expectations. This was illustrated many years ago in the Brooklands Experiment, where sixteen severely subnormal children from a large institution were transferred to a smaller residential unit run on family-group lines. This new environment with its greater frequency and stability of child-adult contacts, coupled with a marked emphasis on individual development, led to improvements in developmental and verbal IQ scores (Tizard, 1964). Further, the large number of mildly retarded persons who appear to function effectively, though at low level, in the community once they escape the labelling process, offers additional confirmation.

Himmelweit and Swift (1969) suggest that it is useful to look at socialization as a series of interlocking experiences in which each successive phase is intimately influenced by the preceding phase. Schooling is one of those phases in which the outcome is partly to define a person's position in society. They further suggest that the phases have differing impacts — that we can look at them in terms of their strength and of how long-lasting are their effects on the individual. For most children the family phase must be regarded as a strong one, and so also must schooling — whether in an ordinary or special school — while for those institutionalized from an early age it is one of the most decisive experiences.

Together with the family, the school is one of the main agents of social learning, and according to Shipman (1968) the process of socialization within schools consists of clear definitions of appropriate behaviour, and rewards and punishments to reinforce it. The process can be seen as a sequence: the first transition from home to school is managed through relaxed informal attitudes, with an emphasis on each individual and a very gradual imposition of simple routines; progressively there will be less personal attention, and there will be rewards for 'mature' behaviour, conformity and cooperation; towards the end of the first school, learning becomes increasingly formal; at the middle or secondary stage pupils are more and more judged on performance rather than personality, there is a decline in expressive activity and an increasing emphasis on instrumental activity. Each part of the sequence has its own norms, rights, privileges and responsibilities.

Arrangements for teaching the handicapped child range from schools within institutions (such as a school for mentally handicapped children within a subnormality hospital), residential schools, day special schools, special units in ordinary schools and full integration within ordinary schools. For disabled children attending ordinary schools socialization must follow the process undergone by their peers although particular disabilities may restrict certain aspects of role learning.

Special schools are particularly interesting since they throw into relief at least two of the points made by Shipman. One of these, like Himmelweit and Swift's concept of strength, is that children are maximally exposed to the culture of their school. Residential schools, and to a lesser extent day special schools, offer such an exposure to new values, attitudes and roles. One consequence of this is to accelerate a disabled child's identification with his disabled peers, who thus become one of his chief reference groups. Within these schools, as in ordinary schools, pupils change in status accorded to their age — with informal structures for younger children and increasing formality for older ones. Since most special schools are small establishments, it is not surprising that they seldom reach the most formal level noted by Shipman where '... surnames replace Christian names ... desks rarely deviate from their columns and rows ... work is more rigidly geared to a syllabus and examinations taken regularly' (Shipman, 1968, p.64), although the selective schools for the most able blind and physically handicapped children are very similar to public schools.

However, the distinctive thing about many special schools is that they continue into adolescence types of instruction not unlike those used with normal pupils in their first schools. The system of one teacher to a class is widespread and, while there is some specialized subject teaching, the juvenile social structure is justified by citing limited mental development, emotional insecurity and poor attainment which together imply the need for the security given by one teacher and a particular classroom. Most children are thought to require the long, personal interaction with a supportive adult that would not take place under more formal arrangements. This pervasive belief also leads to an emphasis on expressive modes of behaviour rather than more instrumental ones.

A government report on 52 schools for delicate pupils illustrates the dilemma of many special schools. It suggests that the caring expressive stance in a small school produces ' ... a consciousness of belonging to a comprehensible community where each child was known and understood, making for contentment in the children who valued the warmth and friendliness of the relationships they experienced' (DES, 1972, p.17). But the reverse side of the coin is that many older children experience a lack of intellectual challenge, that working too slowly leads to under-achievement at school. In one school the kindly atmosphere encouraged those who had been school refusers, but older pupils were described as ' ... immature, dependent, unrealistic and perhaps over-protected'. Whether this problem of reconciling the need for a comprehensible community with academic success and personal and social independence is specific to schools for delicate pupils or whether it applies to other kinds of special schools is open to debate. Lewis (1971) found that pupils in a school for the educationally subnormal had more favourable self-images than pupils of average ability in ordinary schools, and the self-image became even more positive with length of stay; he believed that unrealistically high self-regard could be counter-productive when over-protected pupils were exposed to the rougher realities of post-school life. This point has also been made by Tuckey and Tuckey (1974) in their report on handicapped school-leavers.

In ordinary schools the importance of instruction is readily apparent, and the socialization function coexists with it. Special schools, particularly those dealing with the subnormal and emotionally disturbed, have socialization as their prime objective, and instruction seems to take second place. Further points can, however, be made about special schools. The social milieu created by them and the values which underpin it are in a sense structurally unsupported since the schools often lack a clearly defined community base. If they are residential, their culture may be remote from the children's backgrounds, and the schools may develop quite idiosyncratic values. Of course, to what extent perceptions about the treatment necessary for specific disabilities produce a distinctive social learning environment, is an intriguing question. Those schools for the maladjusted which emphasize behaviour modification, using perhaps token economy systems (where tokens are issued for appropriate behaviour which can be accumulated and exchanged for tangible rewards), presumably have different social consequences for their children than for similar children living in schools where psychotherapy prevails.

6 The family and handicapped children

Family stereotypes

Any general statement about families with handicapped children
should be prefaced by a disclaimer. That is because research on such
families suffers from the same defect that Staples noted in his
review of research on black families. People studying the latter
tended to be white sociologists, with little or no intimate knowledge of the families in question and little or no experience of black
culture, and they examined their evidence in the light of the
predominant model of family life — Anglo-Saxon and middle class.

> The past history of black family research has been characterized
> by the reiteration of unfounded myths and stereotypes ... family
> sociology has a biased value orientation that is reflected in the
> emphasis on middle class norms as the barometer of what is desir-
> able family structure and behaviour. The black family that does
> not meet the criteria of middle class family behaviour is in fact
> defined as a deviant type which should be studied as a patho-
> logical form of social organization. (Staples, 1971, p.119-20)

Studies of families with handicapped children can be criticized for
using images which obscure rather than clarify, images of the family
as a pathological social unit ('in the background of every handicapped child is a handicapped family') or of heroic self-sacrifice —
though both images, over-negative or over-positive, have their

elements of truth. Many such studies lack intimate knowledge, and produce evidence based on limited interviews or highly selective samples. Representative sampling reveals the diversity of parental attitudes, (e.g. by Hewett, 1970; and Gregory, 1976). A more recent trend (Fox, 1974) is to allow the authentic voices of the parents, rather than those of the interviewers, to be heard.

The literature on parental problems has two main approaches. The *practical* approach usually involves facts about family difficulties, e.g. the study of 120 families with a mentally handicapped child by Moss and Silver (1972), who concentrated on such issues as housing, lack of play facilities, holidays, feedings, toilet training, and the extra expense caused by severe handicap. This concern with environmental factors is the hallmark of much British research. However, the *psychological* approach tends to emphasize the emotional reactions of parents and siblings, and seems to be typical of much of the American work in the field. All the same, the difference is one only of emphasis, and most studies do involve both approaches.

Among recent developments in the literature is a recognition of the dynamic change in parental attitudes and reactions in which the child is seen as an active agent. Parallel with this, there has been a growing sensitivity to the social forces which impinge on the family, particularly about how attitudes are shaped and maintained by the reactions of others — neighbours, professionals, the community at large (Voysey, 1975). There has also been an awareness of the impact of the handicapped child not only on the parents but on siblings (Kew, 1975).

A most striking aspect of families with a handicapped child is how vulnerable they are. Their behaviour and attitudes are likely to come under professional scrutiny (these are often interpreted somewhat flexibly according to the research worker's stance). Take, for example, the question of emotional stress. Ross (1964, p.70) suggests that the few controlled studies imply that most parents of the handicapped are under severe emotional stress, while Hewett (1970, p.195) studying parents of children with cerebral palsy found a 'very matter of fact attitude towards the child and the total situation'. Love (1970, pp.27-34) reports parents as suffering shock, refusal, quiet, bitterness, envy and rejection, while Roith (1963, p.51) after working with parents for eight years, found 'the vast majority of parents to be as normal as the parents of ordinary children. Although, as you know, there are some most peculiar parents of ordinary children around.' Roith is quite pungent on the question of guilt feelings and details the ways in which professionals, if determined to find these feelings in parents, can ascribe guilt to any behaviour. (Writing to a hospital for reports on the child's condition implies guilt feelings, while not writing is due to guilt feelings about institutionalizing the child.)

Initial reactions

Whatever the disagreements about family reactions — heroic, rejecting or matter-of-fact — there is widespread agreement that the birth of a handicapped child or the discovery of a defect in early childhood causes a period of profound stress.

When the disability is detected at birth or in early infancy, the responsibility for informing parents usually falls to a paediatrician or general practitioner. The initial reaction is so deeply numbing that parents often cannot grasp more than the most basic facts. They are seldom able to take in the implications and consequences at once. Indeed so severe is the shock that some will deny or reject what has been said to them. There is some evidence that, at least in their recollection, not all parents are given the initial information in a satisfactory way. Tizard and Grad (1961) found that 14 per cent of mothers of mentally handicapped children reported poor handling of cases, and a further 41 per cent reported some unsatisfactory features. Ten years later Moss and Silver (1972) found 44 per cent of their samples expressing dissatisfaction about how they had been told. This is a difficult area to evaluate — retrospective impressions may be faulty; later frustrations due to the child's disability can be attributed to the way parents were initially informed; and methods suitable for one family may not be suitable for another. Sheridan (1973) reveals the other side when she discusses the stress on the doctor, and she notes that 'clinical detachment' can conceal emotional vulnerability. How to tell parents is particularly problematic when, as with spina bifida, their consent to a possible life-saving operation is required at a time when they find it difficult to understand the long-term consequences of their decision (Ellis, 1974).

Not all handicaps are detectable at birth and sometimes those involved only gradually come to suspect that development is not typical. There seem to be two contrasting kinds of response: one is concealment and the other a struggle to get the disability recognized and diagnosed. Younghusband (1970, p.118) reports parents acting as though their child's development were normal and employing strategies to hide their anxieties. Voysey (1972, p.83) quotes the example of one mother who long concealed the real extent of her autistic child's condition, even from her own family. The other response occurs when parents who are worried about aspects of their child's health and behaviour, are dismissed as over-anxious or neurotic, and there are occasions when valuable time is lost through a failure to follow up parents' hunches, as Shepherd (1973) found. As a surgeon, Shepherd complained of the difficulties he had had in getting his deaf child diagnosed. He confessed that his own profession was sometimes prone to give comforting reassurances which led to delays in tackling problems. On balance Shepherd believed that 'it is better that a parent be told of a suspicion of a handicap which may later prove to be ill-founded, than to reassure him and later have the handicap proven' (Shepherd, 1973, p.223).

Whether parents are told skilfully or clumsily, early or late, whether they are tough or tender, this period calls for intensive support, not only in practical day-to-day child care but also in working through the emotions aroused. The connection between initial reaction and subsequent attitudes is rather uncertain.

Types of attitudes

It has been usual to label parental attitudes in terms of broad types which appear to have originated with Somers (1944), studying the personality of the blind adolescent. The classification includes: acceptance, perfectionism, over-protection, and disguised and open rejection. (These are obviously not value-free descriptions.) Acceptance usually refers to the full psychological and social incorporation of the child into the family. Dale (1967) suggested that acceptance ideally involves both parents. Hewett (1970) wrote of the essentially normal family life of children with cerebral palsy. Lowenfeld (1974) found that, while no family was immune to the effects of having a a blind child, many parents were able to accept the child fully.

For Lowenfeld acceptance was more likely when the parents had other, non-handicapped children; when the handicapped child was the first one, acceptance was more difficult. Ross (1964) points out that after the initial crisis many parents develop healthy and constructive attitudes. Occasionally, writers on this subject seem to imply that acceptance is akin to resignation and to a freedom from negative attitudes, but it ought to be positive and to balance special opportunities and attention for the child with a realistic place for him within the family.

Perfectionism, or denial, implies an urge to eradicate the disability, expressed in demanding from the child the full range of normal behaviour. Lowenfeld (1971, p.108) describes perfectionism as the response of parents who love their child but cannot face the reality of his handicap. It is perhaps sustainable while the child is very young, but becomes more difficult when he is of school age. Ross (1964) suggests that where denial takes the form of undue pressure for the achievement of high and unrealistic goals, this leads to frustration, regression and other forms of maladjustment which, while secondary to the main handicap, can have greater impact on the development of the child's personality. This attitude is comparatively rare but is very serious for the individual child.

Those who over-protect are in effect concentrating on the handicap and not on the child. According to Poznanski (1973) this attitude is common among parents. While 'over-protection' cannot be objectively estimated, for Poznanski it means that the handicapped child receives more attention than his disability requires, and much more than any siblings receive. Over-protection limits the child's opportunities for learning independence in habits and ways of thinking, restricts his social interactions and leaves him with little or no chance of coping with feelings of failure. Boone and Hartman (1972) found that over 60 per cent of parents in their samples displayed this 'benevolent over-reaction'. In extreme cases the child's psychological health can only be restored by a period of separation from the family.

Rejection may be concealed by parents who display all the signs of care and concern; in such parents there may be conflict between intellectual and emotional acceptance. Open rejection as Sheridan

(1973) describes it, occurs in two groups of parents — those who are mentally disorded and those who are immature and incapable of assuming their responsibility. However, both groups are thought to be small in number since the overall trend seems to be towards greater acceptance.

The use of such broad terms as 'over-protection' to describe parental attitudes is not without danger. It tends to imply that the attitudes are constant and held equally by both parents. There is a further, though often implicit, assumption that the attitudes stem from the parents' personality. It is more probable that partners do not always have the same attitudes as each other, that attitudes change over the developmental period and are as likely to result from interaction with the child as to be responses to disability *per se*.

Parental attitudes are the product of many forces. Before the birth of a handicapped child, parents are, like all of us, subject to the process of social learning which creates a set of beliefs about disability. Alongside attitudes towards handicap in general, there will be attitudes towards particular kinds of handicap. But perhaps the greatest common source of attitudes is parents' self-blame for their child's condition. An additional factor is the meaning that children have within a marriage. Within the most recent past this has changed since the declining birth rate suggests that parents are more calculating about whether to have children or how many to have. Formerly, couples may have been under some social pressure to have children, and such pressure is to require normal children. Ross (1964) argues that the meaning of children is related to the parents' own childhood. Mothers brought up by critical perfectionist parents are likely to demand perfection of form in their own children, and an imperfect child violates their internalized requirements. Children can be seen as gifts and all gifts have less value if imperfect.

Attitudes and interaction

While there is evidence (Mannoni, 1973) that attitudes and values established in parents before the birth of a handicapped child do influence the way the child is perceived and treated, interactions are most likely to be the potent source of ongoing attitudes. There has been a tendency to ascribe the adjustment or maladjustment of handicapped children to their parents' attitudes. Those parents who were warm and positive had children who were well-adjusted, and disturbed children came from families where they were over-protected or rejected. Like many another basic idea this has its element of truth, but influence is not a one-way street running from parents to children. Walters and Stinnett (1971) suggest that parents' attitudes do change (as the child grows older), and partly because of the nature of the interaction between them and their children. Both parties are engaged in a learning process in which, day by day, expectations are modified, new discoveries made and attitudes progressively change. True, we know little of *how* parents' attitudes are shaped by children's behaviour, but the history of autism is a cautionary tale.

The strange symptoms of autistic children were originally laid at the mother's door. Their extreme withdrawal was seen as a reaction to efficient but detached and remote mothers. Subsequent research has discounted this particular theory — it is plausible that distant, circumspect behaviour in a mother results from years of unaided coping with a withdrawn and uncommunicative child. Park (1972) suggests that the aura of control seen in parents is a defence against the coolness of the professionals they encounter. Hewett (1970, p.111), writing of parents with cerebral palsied children, notes that the mother's behaviour is strongly influenced by the cues supplied by the child and that some of these children are psychiatrically at risk, since during the formation of the mother-child relationship, many of the reward systems which normally reinforce maternal behaviour are not available. Lack of responsiveness in the child means less cues for maternal behaviour. On the other hand, hyperactive children produce an excess of cues, many of them unwanted. Seitz and Terdal (1972, p.40), examining one such case, concluded that the child's high level of activity was maintained by the mother's behaviour in a cumulative spiral of mutual reinforcement. Greater attention should be paid to interaction patterns and strategies for coping than to the grosser labelling of attitudes.

Parental attitudes can also be influenced by membership of organizations specializing in the support of families with a handicapped child. Considering the significance of these organizations, it is surprising that they have not received more attention.

One American study (Katz, 1961) was concerned with parents of children with cerebral palsy, retardation, muscular dystrophy and emotional disturbance. Katz's conclusion was that these self-help groups, whilst providing an outlet for feelings of frustration, also had a socialization role which led to a strong sense of identity with the organization and great deal of voluntary activity — in some cases commitment to the cause was such as to exclude membership of other social groups. Presumably membership of self-help groups influenced attitudes by making parents more familiar with the causes and treatment of a child's condition and with the technical language associated with it, more skilled at dealing with official-dom, and more assured in day-to-day child management. An important aspect of the work of such organizations is the direct instruction of parents in ways of relating to their child and in basic skills, such as encouraging exploration and curiosity in the blind infant and the use of language by the mentally handicapped child.

Three interconnected issues are the relationship between parental attitudes and the adjustment of the children, its impact on academic progress, and the way in which expectations influence patterns of behaviour between parents and children. To illustrate the first, we can consider the study of Neuhaus (1969), who examined the social and emotional adjustment of 84 deaf children. The children in the sample were all of average or near-average intelligence, were without secondary physical handicaps and came from intact families. Attitudes of both mothers and fathers were assessed separately, and the children's adjustment was measured on scales completed by their teachers. Grouping the children into three age bands — 3-7, 8-12 and 13 + — Neuhaus compared adjustment levels with parental attitudes. The mothers' expressed attitudes appeared to be related to adjustment level in all three age bands in the expected direction — positive attitudes coincided with emotional and social stability in the children. The fathers' expres-sed attitudes did not correlate with the adjustment of the younger children, but did influence the older groups. In some cases, it was found that both parents had the same positive or negative attitudes whilst in others each parent held directly opposing attitudes. Positive attitudes in both parents were associated with superior adjustment in the children, and positive maternal and negative paternal attitudes were associated with better adjustment than negative maternal and positive paternal ones. So with this sample and for this disability, maternal attitudes appear to be the more crucial ones for the emotional well-being of the children.

In contrast, Cruickshank (1952) adopted a projective sentence completion test for appraising the effect of family attitudes on 264 handicapped adolescents and a control group. The sentences explored such areas as the family, society, peer groups, other handicapped persons, life goals, fears and guilt. Those sentences that explored the subjects' views of their fathers revealed, amongst the handicapped as well as the non-handicapped, both negative and positive responses, but the handicapped group gave fewer extreme ones. Cruickshank suggests that the more neutral responses of the handicapped show that they are less able to evaluate their relationships with their fathers. Other sentences showed that the handicapped had superior relationships with their mothers than did the non-handicapped, were better able to define these relationships and were secure enough to be more critical. This study, like that of Neuhaus, indicates the value of assessing separately the reactions to mother and father rather than treating them as a coalition. Cruickshank concluded that most handicapped children reported good relationships with both parents, and only by comparison with the control group did some of their anxieties and uncertainties in evaluating relationships with parents stand out.

There have apparently been few studies on the relationships between parental attitudes and the academic achievement of handicapped children, and there are serious problems of method which might explain the reluctance to explore this area. One American study (Rau, 1967) examined the influence of home environment on educable mentally retarded children. Those children who displayed comparatively high achievement had fathers who, when interviewed, more frequently mentioned social and emotional interactions with their children (greeting, talking to, reading to the child) than did the fathers of the other children. Rau also examined the role of parents as teachers and found that mothers of children with low achievement were over-explanatory and verbose. Rau suggested that parents of retarded children need help to become more effective partners with the schools, and the recent work by Hunt (1975) in England with parents of the educationally subnormal shows the value of this approach.

Attitudes and expectations

Attitudes can sometimes be explored obliquely by finding out what expectations parents have for their children. This method has been widely used in connection with handicap. One popular method is to compare the goals and expectations set by parents with those set by a panel of experts or by parents of a matched group of non-handicapped children. Goldman and Shames (1964) studied the goals set by parents of children with a speech defect and found that they were unrealistic (expecting more than was reasonable) about the children's likely progress.

Parental expectations can be a useful starting point for discussing a child's potential and limitations. Barclay and Vaught (1964) compared maternal expectations of cerebral palsied children's future ability to perform certain tasks, with ratings of the children obtained from testing, and concluded that there was a general tendency to over-estimate. A similar finding was made with mothers of retarded children by Heriot and Schmickel (1967). Wolfensburger and Kurtz (1971) compared the judgement of mothers about their retarded children's ability in language, motor skills, intelligence and self-help, with data derived from objective tasks and observation. Most parents were accurate in assessing their children's current abilities — the authors call this 'concurrent realism'. However, when asked to predict adult behaviour and achievement ('predictive realism'), many parents suggested considerable advances which were not thought likely by the professional team who were also making predictions. This poses a difficult problem in human relationships — whether to scale down parents' expectations to what professionals think appropriate or to see these expectations as necessary for maintaining high parental involvement. Wolfensburger and Kurtz note that unrealistic expectations are probably linked with high motivation but that realistic current judgements and predictions cause both parents and child fewer emotional problems. Tew, Laurence and Samuel (1974), in a study of children with spina bifida, found a general but slight tendency in parents to over-estimate future achievements and ability, and this was more marked in parents whose children were in the 60-80

IQ range. Further research will decide whether unrealistically high expectations help or hinder parents and their children.

Attitudes and siblings

So far we have looked at the responses and attitudes of parents. However, other members of the family can be affected by the handicapped child, especially siblings. For some writers, like Martino and Newman (1974), these siblings are at risk of psychiatric disturbance, though others (Caldwell and Gruze, 1960) have found no greater incidence of disturbance in siblings when the handicapped child has remained at home instead of having been placed in an institution. Then again, Holt (1957) showed that about 15 per cent of siblings were adversely affected.

More recently Gath (1973) investigated whether children with a Down's syndrome brother or sister show more psychiatric disturbance than a matched control group. Those children with a sibling with Down's syndrome were the 'index' group, and the control group consisted of pupils from the same school class. Teachers and parents of both groups completed the Rutter Behaviour Scale, a check-list of the frequency of observed behaviours, in which each category of behaviour is selected for its contribution to an overall impression of the child's emotional-behavioural state. Some 10 per cent of the control group were rated as displaying marked deviant behaviour, but the incidence in the index group was 20 per cent. The Rutter Scale allows a distinction to be made between neurotic disorders and anti-social tendencies, and the latter were more frequently seen in the index group, especially among the girls. A suggested explanation is that girls react to demands made on them by the family with deviant behaviour in the classroom. There is implied support for this view in the fact that deviant behaviour is related to family size — small (one Down's syndrome and one normal child) and large; stress in the normal sibling in the small family may be due to the extra burden of parental aspirations. Gath did not discover any specific pattern of deviant behaviour, although she mentioned unpopularity, restlessness and disobedience.

An earlier and somewhat unusual study was that of Shere (1956), who looked at 30 pairs of fraternal twins, one member of each pair having been diagnosed as cerebral palsied. Shere posed several questions: do parents behave differently towards each twin? If they do, can this be evaluated from the standpoint of mental health? Does the handicapped twin behave differently from the other? Parent and child behaviour was assessed during home visits and then the observations were transferred on to rating scales. The general finding was that parental attitudes to the handicapped and non-handicapped twins were broadly similar. Among the differences were a greater understanding of the potential of the cerebral palsied child, and an expectation of a greater degree of responsibility and maturity in the non-handicapped twin than was realistic for its age. Parents appeared sensitive to the problems of the disabled child and less aware of those of the normal one. This was balanced by greater encouragement of independence in the non-handicapped twin, while the disabled one was treated in a rather infantile way. The non-handicapped child seemed to show a greater degree of maladaptive behaviour, whereas the disabled one 'considered himself to be more accepted by the parents and exhibited the behaviour of a secure, accepted child. His non-cerebral palsied twin, however, contrasting the casual acceptance accorded to him with the excessive attention given to his cerebral palsied twin, considered himself rejected and exhibited the behaviour of the insecure, rejected child' (Shere, 1956, p.206). Shere suggests that the non-handicapped child's emotional development is more at risk than that of the handicapped twin.

The age and sex of the siblings seem important. Grailiker *et al.* (1962) found the reactions of teenagers to young mentally handicapped siblings (under 6 years of age) in no way pathological. They led normal active social lives, had warm relationships with their parents and were accepting of their younger retarded brother or sister, since they were secure in their own position within the family. Farber (1959) found that the effect of a severely retarded child depended on the sex of the normal sibling and whether the former was kept at home or placed in an institution. The most disturbing effects were seen in girls when the retarded sibling was kept at home, and in boys when the sibling was placed in an institution. The former was presumed to be due to the amount of care and management of a retarded sibling that falls to a girl, while the behaviour of the boys suggests that following institutionalization they have to cope with demands from parents which were not made before because of a preoccupation with the handicapped child. Lowenfeld (1971, p.210) cautions parents of blind children that the attention given to them can be interpreted by other children as favouritism. Bagley (1971, p.37) noted the evidence on sibling rivalry among children with epileptic brothers or sisters, and a similar observation was made by Dale (1967) about deaf children, especially where hearing brothers and sisters are expected to 'give in' constantly to them. Kew (1975) gives details of the ways in which the attitudes of brothers and sisters to the physically handicapped child are expressed.

The cumulative evidence suggests that it is not invariably true that siblings will be adversely affected by the handicapped child, but that guidance and counselling should not be restricted only to the disabled child and his parents.

No single viewpoint adequately deals with all the issues raised by a family with a handicapped child. At the present time we need to draw upon the insights provided by several disciplines. Among these are the psychoanalytical views, exemplified by the work of Mannoni (1973), who emphasized that the 'dialogue' between mother and handicapped child cannot be comprehended without a profound awareness of the mother's own childhood experience and the symbolic meaning of the child within the marriage coalition.

Psychology can also make a significant contribution, especially with its tradition of precise measurement of parental attitudes through well-standardized attitude scales. The investigation by Cook (1963) using such measures with mothers of blind, deaf, Down's syndrome, cerebral palsied and brain-damaged children suggests patterns of attitudes associated with particular types of handicap, e.g. over-protectiveness with respect to blind children and over-indulgent attitudes to children with hearing problems.

Equally important is the sociological perspective identified with the work of Farber (1959) and his studies of families with severely retarded children. Central to these studies is the concept of the integrated family with its agreement on domestic values and the absence of role-tension in interpersonal relationships. Farber also saw the family as a dynamic social institution which developed through several 'cycles' within which members performed roles with their associated norms and expectations. The presence of a handicapped child, he found, altered the sequential development of the family and radically changed the roles of family members.

Social psychology is a comparative newcomer to this area and we shall accordingly devote rather more attention to its contributions than to those of the disciplines noted above.

Social psychology

Among the interests of social psychology is social interaction. This involves verbal and non-verbal communication. Non-verbal components include gaze direction, posture and facial expression. The complex of behaviour is a 'stream of closely integrated responses subject to continuous correction as a result of feed-back, controlled by more or less conscious plans and subject to partly verbalized rules derived from the culture' (Argyle, 1973, p.14). Social interaction consists of a flow of monitored signals which convey cognitive, emotional and social data. In social interaction, the visibly disabled and the normal are both, initially, unsure of how to respond to each other — the 'rules derived from the culture' are not immediately obvious. Davis (1964) has graphically described some of these social encounters and the sequence of behaviour from fictionalized to real acceptance of the disability and, then, to the maintaining of normal relationships. At the heart of the encounters is the process of impression management; while little is yet known about how the handicapped child learns to carry this out in everyday life, we are beginning to acquire some background on how parents cope.

Parents of visibly handicapped children, though themselves not stigmatized, carry a *courtesy stigma* and occupy an ambiguous social position. 'Their normality is obvious in their performance of conventional social roles; their difference is occasionally manifested by their association with the stigmatized during encounters with normals ... ' (Birenbaum, 1970, p.196). The following groups are, according to Birenbaum, assigned courtesy stigmas: friends or relatives of publicly identified radicals, homosexuals, criminals and mental patients, and parents of handicapped children. They may choose to identify totally with the minority group or to eradicate all evidence of their connection. Between these extremes are those who try to appear to be leading a normal life.

Birenbaum studied the attempts of mothers of retarded children to convey this impression of normality. Their objective was to inform the community that, despite having a retarded child, the family and its members were conventional. Through interviews he sought evidence on how the mothers constructed and maintained a conventional definition of family life. One opportunity for observing this process is when the definition is threatened. The behaviour of the retarded child (at mealtimes or at play with other children) occasionally creates tension for his family, particularly when non-family members are present. The mothers reported that when this occurred, friend were 'considerate', which, when explored, was found to mean a careful ignoring of the handicapped child's behaviour — similar to Davis's 'fictionalized normality'. The normal round of life was further maintained by the family avoiding, whenever possible, situations that would challenge that view. Restricting the retarded child from playing with children in the neighbourhood was one example. Apparently, belonging to a formal organization concerned with mental retardation had an equivocal effect since it increased the family's sense of atypicality, although within the organization, their membership of conventional society was affirmed. In Birenbaum's study, the mothers stressed the similarity of their own to other families in the community, and not to families with a retarded child; this might be increasingly difficult to maintain as the child approaches adolescence and the parents lose the 'capacity to emulate conventional parenthood'.

In a later paper Birenbaum (1971) presents data which suggests that one powerful mechanism by which mothers convey a normal life-style is the development of routines of child management, though such routines may shape maternal attitudes (Cook, 1963). Voysey (1972) argues that in social encounters parents with disabled children are in a 'problematic area' since (i) *definitions of parental competence* are created, and (ii) *the disabled child is less skilful than an adult in social interactions* — is a less reliable role-player — and the competence of the parents is likely to be challenged. In encounters with others, parents will wish to offer *their* definition of their child, his disability and their skills as parents, although the child may be unable to act in harmony with this. 'Thus the claim that a mongol child was "coming on as fast as his brother" was discredited when he made no attempt to hold the cup offered him by the paediatrician...' (Voysey, 1972, p.83).

Voysey contends that two factors, *power* and *responsibility*, significantly modify parents' behaviour. By responsibility she means the extent to which parents, and others, perceive the child's handicap as being caused by the parents (neglect, inadequate care, genetic factors, etc.). Power refers to the extent to which others consider the parent capable of ameliorating the disability or behaviour of the child. These factors are subjective, and they are, as Voysey puts it, 'actors' definitions' and liable to change. She advances four types and their associated parental behaviour:

(1) *Not responsible — with power.* Where the child is 'ill' from a non-hereditary complaint, the parents are able to follow the given medical advice and the predominant interpersonal style is 'coping splendidly'.

(2) *Responsible — with power.* Whatever the objective facts the mother blames herself but is determined to secure the best available treatment. Interpersonal style — 'making amends'.

(3) *Not responsible — no power.* As in some cases of congenital abnormality nothing can change the tragic situation for the parents. They have to manage the expressions of sympathy from others. Interpersonal style — 'stoic acceptance'.

(4) *Responsible — no power.* Where no cause of the handicap can be determined, parents may create their own — as from the mismanagement of the child — but in the case of undifferentiated mental handicap the condition is not remediable. Interpersonal style — 'restricted social interaction'.

The management of social interactions is very important for parents of handicapped children since, through the nature of the handicap, they will meet doctors, teachers, social workers and therapists as well face as the business of impression management in everyday situations. All this involves the growth of sensitivity to others' responses, and skills in handling potentially ambiguous or threatening situations. These skills — Voysey calls them 'competence' — include developing an ability to manage events which would ordinarily by seen as threatening to parental identity; learning to avoid situations where reactions might be uncertain; coping with the 'first time' (the first visit to school, first party, first use of public transport, etc.); and becoming more resilient to slights, rebuffs, insults and mawkish sympathy. 'The skills that parents acquire enable them to typify embarrassing situations and predict alter's response, to define the actions of some categories of others as insignificant and to distinguish true sympathy from mere curiosity' (Voysey, 1972, p.88).

Direct experience

As noted earlier, in a review of sociological research on the black family in America, Staples (1971, p.119) suggested that a good deal of it was 'characterized by the reiteration of unfounded myths and stereotypes'. The investigations had been conducted using white, middle-class norms, although the black family is influenced by quite different social forces. Staples goes further and argues that the research methods were unsatisfactory since some of the researchers lacked direct *experience* of the black family; interviews, question-naires and attitude scales could not fully compensate for this lack.

Some of the literature on parents' attitudes to the handicapped child is incomplete, and even perhaps misleading since it, too, lacks the dimension of experience. Detailed conversations with parents, the completion of attitude scales, and observation itself, these cannot fully admit the investigator to the central experience of living and loving a child with a disability of body or mind. Experience could be critical for reducing simplistic (and often negative) stereotypes of parental attitudes. The courage of parents and children in the face of common stress may contain an element of mystery which is not ultimately reducible to psychological or sociological theory.

7 Schools and handicapped children

Schools as a social system

School is often judged to be one of a child's most formative experiences. When that experience is somewhat unusual, the consequences might well be unlike those of conventional schooling. We are not here going to examine the evidence (such as it is) for the educational effectiveness of the schooling of handicapped children, but to suggest which aspects of their experience, whether in ordinary or special schools, are important in estimating its overall effect. To do this, we require a general framework, and the one which seems to have the widest applicability is that proposed by Willower (1970).

Willower argued that a social-system perspective, such as the one described by Getzels (1952), suitably modified might be a useful starting point for examining special education. He commented, as several others have, on the excessive reliance on psychological and medical views of handicapped children and their development. Social psychological interest in this area was new at the time and could provide an antidote. In applying a 'social psychological perspective' to special education, Willower suggested a threefold approach which included: (i) the nature of the organizations within special education; (ii) their characteristics as social systems; and (iii) the relationship between small and large organizations — such as between a special class and the host school or between special schools and ordinary schools.

Each relatively stable component could be studied to find the roles and expectations both of and for participants, the pattern and nature of authority in formal as well as in informal systems, the process of socializing new members and the personal consequences for participants. Willower suggests as an example of relationships between organizational structures, the referral system by which children are recommended by an ordinary school for a place in a special school. This is not the only way in which children are referred since it can be done by parents direct, by doctors, social workers and others. When children have obvious defects, this is known well before school age, but numerous children are referred by ordinary schools and many of these will have learning and/or behaviour problems. The referral chain often consists of a class-teacher recognizing that a child has marked learning or adjustment problems and communicating this to the headteacher, who then makes arrangements with the School Psychological Service for an examination. The views of the class-teacher and headteacher are taken in conjunction with the psychologist's evidence. If special school placement is considered, then parents are brought into the discussion early on.

For Willower the referral process is not just one of applying precise educational or psychological criteria. The referring school, like all organizations, is concerned with survival — even more so when the organization is relatively stable. One measure of stability is the degree to which the school has control over pupils who threaten the *status quo*. Within its own confines the school usually has a number of methods available for dealing with pupils who challenge stability — to place them in a special class or unit where educational or behavioural deviance can be legitimized, to exclude or transfer them to another school, or to define their problems in such a way as to make them someone else's concern. Children who are referred can then be regarded as heterogeneous threats to organizational stability rather than as members of clinically well-defined categories. Within its own confines the school can disperse children with a fair degree of autonomy but in the referral process the school psychologist acts as a deterrent to unrestricted offloading.

All this explains much of the diversity of attainments and characteristics reported in samples of educationally subnormal and maladjusted pupils since their deviance cannot be fully taken into account by psychometric data. Schools are not unaware that referral and placement can be made easier by expressing a child's problems in terms which legitimate his removal. For Willower the evidence that placement is a part of an institutional response to pupil opposition is to be found in the contrast between the intense efforts and complex procedures for placement, and the attempts made to return pupils from special schools. The elaborate mechanism for removing pupils as against the informal approach to reintegrating them indicates the respective values the institution places on these activities. The procedures are more than devices for responding to perceived needs in children, they are institutionalized practices for getting rid of organizational irritants.

White and Charry (1966) show how the social background of pupils referred to school psychologists appears to influence the diagnostic labels applied to them by their teachers, and also how social class seems to be connected with the type of action and the quality of resources available. Middle-class children enjoy greater access to more expensive and scarcer resources; working-class children have remedial teachers, while middle-class ones are sent to psychiatrists. Mercer (1971) followed the chain of referral for retarded pupils from different ethnic backgrounds, and found that as the process moves from referral to special class placement, so there is a corresponding significant increase in the proportion of ethnic-minority children punitively misclassified. The percentage of children from the West Indies in schools for the educationally subnormal, shows the same trend (Coard, 1971). This is not to imply that the referral-placement procedure is exclusively a matter of deliberately offloading troubled and troublesome pupils, with the help or collusion of the School Psychological Service, but rather than the procedure is unlike the precise identification and treatment of a communicable disease, since the organizational context is a factor in the decision-making process. (Woolfe (1977) describes this process at work in the definition of maladjusted pupils.)

As an example of the 'characteristics of social systems within special education', Willower considers the teachers of handicapped children as a subculture. While he offers little in the way of evidence to justify this concept, he does suggest several questions: do those who choose to teach the handicapped have particular personal characteristics? What is the process by which a teacher defines himself as a 'special educator' and does this imply a change in professional group from 'teacher' to 'special teacher' or to 'teacher of the blind or the deaf'? Tobin (1972) found that only a minority of a sample of teachers in training expressed a willingness to teach the handicapped, and these in turn showed clear differences in willingness to teach different kinds of handicapped children. Sharples and Thomas (1969) discovered that teachers of handicapped children attributed greater prestige to their own specialism than did teachers in other specialisms; this suggests that there are narrowly defined professional groups. Gottfreid and Jones (1970) examined the job-satisfaction of teachers of the retarded and related this to their perceptions of personal need-satisfactions found in teaching. They noted that job-satisfaction went along with a teaching role which legitimized a combination of personal and professional need-gratification. The teacher subculture is not the only social system that could be explored — others are pupil-teacher roles, patterns of power and authority within schools and informal social relationships.

A third and final example from Willower is the behaviour of those who are labelled as different. Specifically he points to the paucity of studies on the coping behaviour of those singled out for special education. This behaviour appears to have several components — self-esteem, impression management and styles of adjustment. We may catch something of what Willower has in mind here when we find senior pupils from a day special school for the educationally subnormal pretending they attend a nearby comprehensive school (denial of stigma), or when we consider Edgerton's (1963) study of a group of adolescents in an institution who by their distinctive clothes, their attachment to the youth culture outside the institution, their particular and exclusive in-group language and their resistance to conformity affirmed that they belonged to the wider peer group and rejected a categorization that denigrated them (counter-affirmation of normal identity). Impression management may be seen in Harrison's (1976) work on epilepsy; he found that the mortification of stigma was coped with by defining an epileptic seizure as 'an occasional blackout' or a 'dizzy spell' (naturalistic explanation).

The ground plan suggested by Willower seems to have

considerable potential for exploring the effects of special education on handicapped pupils as well as opening up many aspects of the organizations and professional groups within it.

Acceptance of handicapped children at school

From a social point of view, perhaps the central issue in the schooling of handicapped children is the manner and extent of their acceptance as members of their class at school. This acceptance will include the behaviour of teachers and classmates, and where both adults and others have the same positive attitudes, it is likely to be easier, quicker and more firmly based. The disabled child attending his or her first school may still have difficulties even when the attitudes are uniformly positive, since this may be the first time that contrasts in functional capabilities vividly show up.

Fishman and Fishman (1971) noted a three-part process through which a disabled child passes, and describe it as a series of confrontations between him and his disability. At the cognitive level he will wish to understand his disability, its causes and prognosis. Emotional confrontation occurs when he feels able to express his feelings about it, especially negative ones, although there may be taboos on expressing them overtly. Interpersonal confrontation is when he is able to talk to peer group members about his disability, its existence is publicly acknowledged and it is incorporated into his social identity without stigma.

The combination of accurate information, emotional confrontation and communication with his peer group implies a degree of openness to the totality of the disabled child's problems. However, his presence in an ordinary classroom, if it is only symbolic of a more 'progressive' attitude to disability, is unlikely to open up this process of confrontation. Equally, when teachers and children are ambivalent in attitude, the disabled child's emotional needs may be concealed by treating him 'just like anyone else'. For teachers and children the task is to attend simultaneously both to disablement and to normality. It may be an effective social lubricant to smooth over awkward problems with a simple undemanding bonhomie.

More serious, obviously, is the effect on handicapped pupils of dislike and rejection. Anderson (1973) noted that many mildly handicapped pupils in primary schools experienced few overt expressions of dislike and that in general disabled children were well accepted. Minde and his colleagues (1972) investigated the psycho-social development of a group of physically handicapped pupils and found that the younger children regarded themselves as non-handicapped but as having a functional limitation which was 'external' to them as persons, and that they believed in a positive prognosis. Transfer to a special school with many others similarly handicapped brought on a period of profound melancholy because of separation from home combined with being in a milieu which made it explicit that the handicap was by no means certain to be alleviated. In time this confrontation with their disability was partly resolved since the children acquired a view of themselves and their future which included their disability. Thus, we see that acceptance has the dual aspects of both recognition by significant other people and self-recognition of limitations.

It is hardly possible to exaggerate the importance of the teacher's role in helping the disabled child to adjust to his handicap and in assisting other children to accept it, either through personal example or by modifying attitude more directly. Marge (1966), in a study of the social acceptance of speech-handicapped pupils in ordinary schools, discovered that pupils' and teachers' attitudes to the handicapped were similar, and that both expressed a strong preference for the non-handicapped. Children are such acute observers of their teachers that it would be surprising if there were not a link between their own and their teachers' attitudes; the positive ones observed by Anderson (1973) may be interpreted in this way. Thomas and Yamomoto (1970) used a semantic differential scale, a method devised for the 'measurement' of the meaning of words or constructs, to investigate the attitudes of three groups of emotionally disturbed children. They found that on the merit dimension they ranked their class teachers next to their parents; and the significance of their teachers to them did not decline with the onset of adolescence.

It is not easy to obtain accurate information about the acceptance of the disabled child at school. Observation would seem to be the most reliable method, but by far the most popular research approach is to use sociometry. This attempts to quantify the relative status of children in groups through such questions as, 'Who is your best friend?' 'Who would you like to sit next to?' Much effort has been put into establishing the validity and reliability of sociometric methods (e.g. Evans, 1962), and despite their evident disadvantages, they can clarify the patterns of friendships, groupings and isolation within a class. Among the reported findings (Rucker, Howe and Sniden, 1969) is that slow-learning children in integrated classes have a lower social status and presumably are less well accepted than other children. A related issue is the extent to which children accorded low status on an anonymous questionnaire are aware of the feelings of others towards them. It seems that slow-learning or retarded children are inclined to over-estimate their social standing in a class group. Mallenby (1973, 1974) has explored whether their perception of their status is due to being unable to read the signs of acceptance or rejection, or whether their true status is known but denied. Compared with more severely retarded children, mildly retarded ones, especially boys, tended to be much more distant with adults, and this was taken as evidence of growing awareness of low status and low acceptability.

Among the factors which might influence acceptance is how visible the disability is. Adams and Cohen (1974) found that on first encountering a new group of children, teachers were influenced by their appearance and physique but that these external characteristics soon became less and less significant in the teachers' evaluations. Children's attitudes to a disabled child must surely develop similarly: while the visibility of the affliction may be very important for initial acceptance or rejection, it may become progressively less important provided there are opportunities for social interaction. Functional disabilities are probably central for younger children evaluating their peers, while for older ones, social stigma may be more crucial.

Richardson, Ronald and Kleck (1974) observed the behaviour of normal and disabled children at a summer camp, and found visibility of defect to be one variable contributing to the low social status of the disabled; nor did its significance decrease during the camping period. Of the normal children, 54 per cent were evaluated positively by their peer group, 10 per cent neutrally and 36 per cent negatively. Of the handicapped with non-visible defects, 46 per cent were evaluated positively, 8 per cent neutrally and 46 per cent negatively. For the visibly disabled the percentages were 40, 16 and 48 respectively. However, it does seem from these figures that visibility of handicap is not as significant a factor, taken by itself, as it might at first appear. Richardson and his colleagues therefore considered that in addition peer-group status is influenced by the handicapped child's skill in interpersonal relationships, and from their observations concluded that many of the handicapped were inadequately equipped in this connection.

Other factors likely to influence acceptance of the handicapped schoolchild are: practical communication difficulties; episodic conditions; competence; atypical behaviour; level of interpersonal skills; and frequency of contact. Speech or hearing problems are likely to be amongst the factors that will make acceptance harder to achieve, although the difficulties encountered in class will make both teachers and children aware of this potential source of social isolation. Less overt but perhaps no less significant is the area of interpersonal skill that Richardson noted. Bilsbury and Bromley (1974) found that 'withdrawn' educationally subnormal pupils gave more impoverished responses in a person-perception interview than did more outgoing children in the same category, and they suggested that this may be because the withdrawn child, with his limited social experiences, has fewer and simpler impressions of others on which to draw. Awareness of the complexity of others as social stimuli is one of the skills required for successful social behaviour. Here again, observation of handicapped children's behaviour in social settings is probably the best starting point for investigation, but something may be achieved by using simulated social behaviour.

Weiss and Weinstein (1968) compared the verbal tactics employed by institutionalized and non-institutionalized retarded persons towards target persons — 'best friend' and 'authority figure'. One of their probes was to ask subjects to imagine that they were intending to watch a favourite television programme only to find that their best friend was already watching something else. They were asked how they would get the friend to change programmes, and also why their suggested tactic would work. Both groups seemed to favour relatively unsophisticated tactics, such as just asking, but the institutionalized group was somewhat more subtle. This was ascribed to the latter's experience of living in an environment with few personal rewards, while the home-based group was thought to be over-protected and to have found that the simple tactic of asking was sufficient to get them what they wanted.

Holden and Thomas (1976) investigated educationally subnormal and normal pupils' responses to the same probes; they found little difference in the tactics or rationale of either group, and concluded that the questions themselves prompted the use of unsophisticated tactics, although the normal sample was more sensitive to the needs and attitudes of the other person.

One aspect of interpersonal skill is impression management. Braginsky and Braginsky (1972) discovered that retarded youngsters could manipulate their IQ test scores within certain limits, depending on whether they saw the outcome of the testing as positive or negative. This suggested that if subjects could manipulate supposedly intractable material like IQ tests, then most probably they could be effective in other areas of impression management. However, there is evidence that some handicapped children cannot create and maintain satisfactory levels of social acceptance. Laing (1972) reviewed the sociometric studies of educationally subnormal children and concluded that whilst their social life had many of the features observed in sociometric studies of normal children, a proportion of pupils in special schools lacked those social skills which make for acceptance or popularity. This was partly due to the large number with behaviour disturbance and partly to the school's practice of rapidly switching children from group to group in order to maintain uniform pupil-teacher ratios. One would have thought that special schools, as caring communities, would be more concerned with the children's socio-personal development than with organizational equity.

Evans (1962, pp.40, 55) has pointed out that the teacher should be more concerned with the child who seeks friendship but cannot find it, than with notions of popularity. Friendship can often make all the difference between liking or loathing school. Psychologically, friendship is an elusive concept, and definitions such as 'attenuated sexual relationships' or 'reciprocal need satisfactions' are inadequate. Two examples will serve to illustrate the value of friendship among the handicapped. MacAndrews and Edgerton (1966) recount the friendship of Lennie and Ricky, who were in an institution for many years, and were both severely handicapped. It has lasted for ten years and was non-sexual, non-exploiting, warm, and supportive, though exclusive. Joseph Deacon in his autobiography (1974) describes how through friendship with another patient, he found the one person who could understand and interpret his speech. Obviously, close friendship cannot be manufactured for children, but perhaps there is a place for developing social skills that make it more likely.

Gaining social acceptance within a group or forming deeper relationships are related to the norms of behaviour within the group. One obstacle to acceptance is behaviour which conflicts with those norms. Episodic conditions like epilepsy cause anxiety and uncertainty both in the epileptic child and in others relating to him. Anderson (1973) found that while disabled children in ordinary schools had a somewhat lower sociometric status than non-handicapped peers, much of the variance could be accounted for by the handicapped with neurological abnormalities or a combination of disabilities — for example, cerebral palsy plus very low attainment resulted in lower status. This is reminiscent of the work of Jacobs and Pierce (1968), who compared retarded children with and without neurological abnormalities and found that the ancillary characteristics of the latter — perceptual difficulties, poor motor coordination, hyperactivity, limited attentiveness, impulsiveness and emotional lability (mood changes) — were closely and cumulatively associated with lower social status. Acceptance is modified by socially unacceptable behaviour. While adults may be tolerant of bizarre behaviour, it puzzles other children and challenges their emerging concepts of acceptable patterns of behaviour.

Acceptance is increased or diminished by perceptions of competence, either academic or physical. Gottlieb and Davies (1973) tried to examine this factor by arranging for normal and retarded children in an integrated or segregated school setting to select a partner for a skilled motor task, and found that children of average mental ability selected significantly fewer retarded children as partners. Willey and McCandless (1973) used checklists of adjectives to study the reciprocal perceptions of groups of normal, retarded and orthopaedically handicapped children, and discovered that both the normal and the retarded ascribed more positive terms to their own group than to the other group, though retarded pupils (in special classes) expressed somewhat more positive attitudes towards normal peers than were reciprocated. The authors suggest that the retarded seemed to be unaware of the normals' denigrating attitudes towards them. Perceptions of the orthopaedically handicapped by these 8-12 year-old pupils were almost wholly positive, perhaps because they felt inhibited about expressing attitudes to the disabled or saw them only in stereotyped, though positive, ways. This occurred in school settings which encouraged a good deal of contact between the groups, and proximity has long been thought to be an important factor in the forming of friendships since it fosters initial acquaintance. However, Gottlieb and Davies (1973) were studying retarded and normal pupils in an open-plan school, a setting which presumably gives most opportunities for social interaction, but found that while other children were highly aware of the retarded ones, this did not improve the acceptance and status of the latter.

Special schooling

Educational provision for the handicapped is a continuum extending from acceptance and integration within an ordinary school at one pole to institutionalization at the other, with special classes, day special schools and residential special schools lying in between. This variety illustrates in concrete terms the duality of attitudes to handicap — the desire to create some positive means of assistance and the willingness to separate and confine. Separate education for groups with common medical or psychological characteristics was also a necessary first step in providing for those for whom there was previously little or no education at all, as well as a convenient way of concentrating scarce resources on pupils who were spread over a wide area. Furthermore, it actively met the need to make some kind of egalitarian gesture by which educational opportunities available to the broad mass of children could also be seen to be there for their less fortunate brothers and sisters.

Yet again, we may see the development of special schools as a further example of one of the dominant themes of British education — the philosophy and practice of classifying, sorting and grouping children. In this there is both a sorting-out and a sorting-in process. The sorting-out process did, and does, give statutory and moral support to the concept of limited variability: schools appear to have a view of the range of children's physical, mental and behavioural characteristics with which it is reasonable to expect them to cope. Special schools embody the principle that ordinary schooling is for those who fall within the restricted variability of behaviour and development which schools establish for themselves. The sorting-in process is one which classifies and places children according to criteria which are increasingly subject to controversy (Whitmore, 1975).

It can be argued that special schools by their openness — bring me your blind, crippled and retarded children and I will cherish them — have, as they have grown, provided a validating system for ordinary schools to narrow their version of what are acceptable pupils. This problem has its reverse side, however, since special schools also have their own ideas about their rightful clients, and because pupils do not always show easily classifiable symptoms, judgements about which educational system, ordinary or special, is right for a particular child, give rise to endless boundary disputes. The elaborate classification of children by physical or behavioural characteristics following the 1944 Education Act has increased rather than decreased the intensity of this insular and self-perpetuating debate. Trying to find a special school place for a 14-year-old girl who suffers from epilepsy, maladjustment and serious educational retardation, means experiencing it at first hand.

The controversy about whether there is or is not anything special about special schools, has gone on for a long time (Lumsden, 1966). Clearly they represent, in an extreme form, the general view that schools are largely composed of persons in involuntary relationships with each other. Children are usually selected and placed in special schools when it is thought that little or no advantage can be gained from ordinary schools. Normally, though by no means always, these pupils have certain defects of mind or body which distinguish them from those of similar age in ordinary schools. The schools themselves are small — although there are a handful with over 200 pupils and one or two with 300, some have as few as 39 and many an average of around 100 pupils. While some are single-sex, most are mixed, and often admit pupils of all school ages. These are drawn from a wide area — sometimes from the whole country — and even day special schools take pupils from a larger area than comparable primary or secondary schools. The manner of instruction is also different — either there are special teaching methods, e.g. for the blind or deaf, or the teacher-pupil ratio is likely to result in the handicapped child being taught in a small group; and many special schools use the traditional primary-school method of one teacher being responsible for teaching a wide range of subjects to his or her class. Medical and para-medical staff and the treatment they bring with them are also a distinctive feature.

Special schools have several aims for their pupils, and these aims extend across medical and educational categories. They include making the exceptional as normal in behaviour as possible. This can mean, for example, the training of the subnormal in basic everyday skills, the teaching of oral communication to the deaf, the mobility training of the blind and the medical treatment of the disabled. Here, there is the common purpose of enabling the child to blend into his social context as far as possible. A second general aim is the vital notion of independence — the maximum economic, social and personal self-sufficiency for the child. Many handicapped children appear to achieve both these aims. A third one is 'accommodation', i.e. helping the child or young person to live with disability in a way that minimizes its handicapping effect. The disabled child has sufficient problems without extra psychological hang-ups. Finally, special schools often have an implicit aim of avoiding the effcts of special schooling itself. Most of them are aware that the milieu they create is itself not wholly conducive to their explicit aims. Admission to special schools can seldom be regarded as an act which brings much pleasure to any of the parties involved. The argument about integration and segregation has its historical aspect dating back to the time when children were certified as 'defective', physically or mentally — certified as unfit for the company of their fellows — and some of the stigma of placement remains today; thus, Voysey (1972) can write of the 'mortification of special schooling'.

Among the effects of segregated schooling on the handicapped children are: (i) it places them in a social system largely composed of others similarly handicapped, so that they take the others as their reference group; (ii) particularly when it is residential, it means a loss of contact with normal peer groups and all that that implies for psychological and social development; (iii) the children lose friendships in their home neighbourhood; (iv) there is the sense of stigma; (v) a too-protective environment is dangerous because of the effect of the loss of protection when the young people have to leave it; (vi) there are the consequences of a school environment which is uncertain whether it is a branch of the social services, a para-medical aid centre or a teaching institution. However, there are also positive features: (i) a high ratio of adults to children and the greater attention which individual children can then receive; (ii) the efficiency of special instructional methods; (iii) the concentrated availability of medical and therapy services, (iv) the reduction of pressure on children which gives them the opportunity and time to cope with physical self-care and the psychological opportunity to build up worthwhile levels of self-esteem; (v) the living in a comprehensible community where needs are acknowledged and catered for.

Rackham (1975) suggests that many people will find it strange that schooling is an integral part of the treatment, since we have become used to regarding treatment and education as distinct processes that take place in different kinds of establishments with different regimes and different roles. She considered residential education in relation to three disorders: diabetes, epilepsy and asthma or eczema. These three conditions are similar in that, given the right treatment and good management, they can most probably be controlled, if not cured. Rackham notes the beneficial effect on young patients when this problem is handled by sympathetic and competent doctors and nurses, and she contrasts the attitudes of the knowledgeable and skillful doctors with those of such parents as display panic and anxiety when faced with an asthmatic attack or an epileptic seizure. Young children with these disorders who start day school at five years of age, have the double handicap of a new role without family support if a crisis occurs. Even such apparently innocuous things as using an inhaler or taking medicine regularly can cause unease, and they may be anxious about how other children will react to their special needs. There are problems in getting children with these handicaps to school, and so parents may tend to keep them away for fear that any stress will bring on another attack.

... the picture is of children with a constitutional disorder largely controlled by appropriate medical treatment with only occasional overt physical manifestations requiring specific treatment. The disorder creates an atmosphere of anxiety in the sufferer and his family resulting in stress and a tendency to over-protect or reject on the part of the parents, and to withdraw from involvement in normal childhood activities, or become aggressively anti-social, on the part of the child. School attendance tends to be irregular, resulting in a falling behind in achievement and a sense of failure, and there is often exclusion from group activities leading to isolation. (Rackham, 1975, p.25)

Children with episodic conditions need care at three levels: medical, psychological and educational. Medical treatment means regular supervision and immediate attention in a crisis; they need an 'atmosphere of relaxed assurance' and, at school, a chance to catch up and to have opportunities for academic success and involvement in group activities. These needs can be met within a boarding school, where both skilled medical supervision takes place and learning is promoted in a milieu of relaxed assurance. Attendance improves — Rackham says from between 25 and 75 per cent before admission, to 95 per cent afterwards. Boarding schools of the 'five day' variety, where children can go home at weekends, are probably the best for them.

Rackham notes that boarding schools do create difficulties — contact with families is reduced, friendships in the home neighbourhood are lost, the parents' share in their children is less, and development is slower. She suggests boarding school placement (i) where there is a severe or persistent medical condition and even with medical and social-work support the family is unlikely to meet the child's needs; (ii) where school attendance or progress is retarded by the condition or by lack of suitable management within the home. The antagonism to separate special schools is such that in Rackham's view a rational argument for the positive contribution of such establishments is difficult to make at present. Very similar arguments to those advanced by Rackham for asthmatic and epileptic children can be put forward for children whose emotional or behavioural problems stem from domestic tensions and conflicts, and for them boarding schools would also still seem to offer selective advantages.

Institutionalization

As Tizard and Tizard (1974) noted, in developed countries

a sizeable percentage of children spend part or the whole of their childhood in residential institutions. In 1963, of an estimated child population of 11.5 million, 146,500 (1.3 per cent) were deprived of normal home life — there were 78,000 in the care of local authorities and voluntary agencies, 15,000 protected children in foster homes, 10,000 delinquent children in approved schools, 24,000 handicapped children in special boarding schools and 19,000 handicapped children in hospital or subnormality units. Tizard estimated that something around 80-90,000 were long-stay cases spending 'the whole of their childhood in establishments staffed by paid professional staff and organized in a manner very different from that of an ordinary home or foster home', and we might add, organized in a different way from special residential schools. Institutions of this kind have an important role in the care of handicapped children, but the social and psychological consequences of long-stay care for the development of children need to be examined, not only to compare them with children brought up at home, but also in terms of differences of organization, attitudes and social climate between institutions.

Although these institutions have continued to provide a basic rescue service for unwanted and neglected children, much has been written in both Britain and America on the damaging effects of their regimes. Institutions for children share in the opprobrium which has attached itself to those for adults. Changes in public policy and better social supportive services have attempted to reduce the number of children requiring institutionalizing but, as with fostering, have not eliminated the problem. Among the trends noted by Tizard has been the breakdown of large barrack-like institutions into smaller homes and — equally significant — the improvement in the number and quality of establishments for infant and pre-school children. But there is still room for progress and they suggest that subnormality hospitals and some long-stay units for children with other handicaps, are not providing care comparable in quality with that given by the smaller establishments for deprived children. However, despite the major changes in child care policy a negative image of institutional life persists in the public mind.

The central problem in the long-term care of handicapped children is that they are developing persons, more vulnerable than adults, dependent on adults for care and protection and presumably more at risk of physical and psychological trauma. One of the main contributions of Tizard was to illuminate the variety of social climates and organizational patterns in institutions for the mentally handicapped child. This included the measuring of the quality and frequency of child-adult interaction, how this related to organizational factors, and their combined influence on the development of individual children. They found differences in child management between the child-oriented small hostel and the large mental hospital whose care was institution-oriented, and they noted that these differences were not due to children's handicaps but to size and organizational ethos, though there were other factors involved such as the nature of the staff-training. In child-oriented units, children were superior in self-help skills when compared to children in the other units.

Further studies explored the quality of relationships of very young mentally handicapped children in nursery units, and of those at home — the latter showed 'strong attachement to the mother while the attitudes of nursery children was more diffuse', as might be expected given the comparatively large number of adults with whom they came into contact. Tizard is optimistic that the lack of a deep single attachment in very young children does not inevitably lead to a failure to develop properly. Healthy development can occur without specific attachments, but multiple care (shared by many adults) means instability and, when taken to extremes — is hardly conducive to good results.

In the 1971 White Paper, *Better Services for the Mentally Handicapped*, the continuance of the long-term hospital was questioned and hostel accommodation within the community was suggested as the positive alternative. But the hospitals are still a reality despite criticism that institutional efficiency is sometimes put before the needs of individual patients, and that institutional care in a sense deprives the child or adult of their birthright to be part of the general community. (See Miller and Gwynne (1974) for a stimulating appraisal of residential institutions.)

Conclusion

Haffter's survey (1968) of European folklore of the Middle Ages reminds us that in our society positive attitudes to the handicapped are of recent origin. Keith Thomas (1977) has shown how in Tudor and Stuart England, a significant element in popular humour was directed at the eccentric and the deviant, at foreigners (the Welsh were the Irish then if you will forgive the Irish!) and at the deaf, the lame and the blind. He charts how aristocratic manners and Puritan reticence led to

> a growing conviction that man should not be mocked for unavoidable misfortunes and that deformity and suffering were matters for compassion not laughter. No such inhibitions had been found in the jest-books where every disability from idiocy and insanity to diabetes and bad-breath was a welcome source of amusement. 'We jest at a man's body that is not well proportioned,' said Thomas Wilson, 'and laugh at his countenance if it be not comely by nature.' ... such humour reflected the actual practice of a world where most professions were closed to the deformed and where visits to Bedlam were a standard form of entertainment and where idiots were maintained in noble houses for amusement's sake....

The new sensitivity and sensibility was such that by the end of the eighteenth century 'the doctrine that human weakness was no subject for laughter had taken hold of middle-class opinion', and it is from this that we may trace the humanitarian and philanthropic movements of the next century. Thomas concludes:

> As for the softening of laughter, the discontinuance of the household fool and the banning of jokes about madness or deformity, we approach an area which has not lost its sensitivity. For there are some matters which even *we* regard as privileged from jest.

By the beginning of the nineteenth century, there was a growing interest in both philosophical and psychological speculation about the blind, the deaf and the insane, along with a small but growing body of experience derived from the first experiments in care, treatment and education. We may catch the spirit of this speculation in a review (*Galignani's Literary Review*, 1821) of an essay on the instruction and assessment of the blind.

> The want of sight not only deprives the blind of the sensations which that organ gives to those who have sight, but also extends its influence over all their thoughts, which it modifies and distorts; all their ideas, therefore, are false or contrary to the notions we have; it is blindness which plunges them in the ignorance in which they are of decorum, and which deprives them of the sentiment of social decencies. Modesty, which is one of the graces of youth, is to them almost an imaginary being, though they have a sort of timidity, which, it is true, belongs perhaps rather to fear than to shame, but which greatly augments their embarrassment in certain circumstances.
>
> Unfortunate in all their relations with other men, they are very imperfectly acquainted with those emotions which draw us towards each other, and decide our affections and attachments. Sensibility has not, for them, those charms which make us place it in the rank of the sweetest as well as the most amiable virtues. Unhappy creatures! their situation, which forces them to be on their guard against all the world, makes them often place in the same class their benefactors and their enemies; and without meaning it, perhaps, they appear ungrateful. It is these motives which make them form connections with the blind rather than with those who have sight, whom they consider as a different class of beings. Is it that they apprehend our inconstancy, or distrust our superiority, or else find more points of association among each other?

They will easily be excused, when we reflect on the number of signs that are lost to him who is deprived of sight. Those external motions, which are painted so expressively on the countenance, that faithful mirror of the soul, do not exist for them. They are continually, in their relations with other men, as one is with an individual whom one knows only by correspondence, we know perfectly well that he exists, but we cannot conceive how.

If not very open-hearted, on the other hand, nature gives them an ample compensation by endowing them with a prodigious activity of imagination and an insatiable desire of knowledge which in them, is a substitute for many affections that they want, or at least for the expansion which such sentiments might have. This state of their imagination banishes ennui, which is one of the least inconveniences of blindness; for we meet with very few blind persons who have not formed some sort of occupation for themselves, and with complete success.

Obliged to judge of men and things intrinsically, they must necessarily obtain truer results than us; moreover, as I have repeatedly said, they see things in a more abstract manner than we, and in questions of pure speculation are less subject to be deceived; for abstraction consists in separating in thought the sensible qualities of bodies from each other, and error commonly springs from a defective separation. They have no need, like us, to guard themselves against the illusions of the senses, since they cannot be seduced by appearances: the charms of the countenance, the richness of clothes, the sumptuousness of apartments, the dignity of office, and the prejudice attached to birth, are nothing to them: it is the moral man who they appreciate. How much more certain must their judgements be, in this respect, than ours?

A soft and sonorous voice is to them the symbol of beauty. They know, pretty exactly, by the compass of the voice, what is the stature and size of the person who speaks, the largeness of the room they happen to be in, etc. But with what nicety of discernment must these attentive observers judge, by this means, of the temper and of certain shades of character which escape us, becuase we have not the same interest in remarking them?

Their self-love, which is the most prominent of all their

defects, and, perhaps, the origin of all the others, is compensated by some valuable qualities; their invincible patience and extreme tenacity in their enterprises render them capable of surmounting the greatest obstacles without ever being disheartened.

In 1890 the reporter of the *Blackburn Times* (30 August, 1890, quoted by Fothergill, 1977) could begin an article on the blind entitled 'What should be done for them? what can they do for themselves? in the following way: 'Happily there is in all classes general sympathy with the blind, and the neglected condition in which so large a proportion are found is owing principally to ignorance of what to do, and how to do it .... ' The transformation from objects of ridicule to object of compassion is a remarkable one, but of course such public sentiments were less readily available to other disabilities.

Drimmer (1976) describes the public appetite for exhibitions of human 'freaks and oddities'. His account of the use of persons with gross deformities arouse conflicting emotions — revulsion at the Roman Holiday mentality that could turn deformity into a commercial venture, and admiration for the human curiosities who fashioned a worthwhile life for themselves in the tolerant and accepting community of the circus. It is no exaggeration to write of the attitude change towards the disabled as a social revolution in which their status has altered from discrimination, to derogation through custodial and philanthropic concern, and on towards the goal of integration. Recent reports like that of Court (1976), and the Snowdon Working Party (1976) are examples of attempts to establish structural social changes which will remove the final vestiges of physical, economic or social barriers. Such reports sharply remind us that progress is slow and uneven — the status of the mentally handicapped and of those with the graver forms of epilepsy is not yet equivalent to that, say, of the blind. As well as the necessity for right kind of social, economic and supportive services, there is the ever-present need to break down interpersonal barriers.

Alongside the basic structure of legislation, health, housing, jobs and care, which increasingly involves central and local government, there is the phenomenon of the growing involvement of concerned people expressing their wish to help the handicapped, either through voluntary societies or simply as individuals, and among them are many young men and women. They do not wish to play the outdated Lady Bountiful, but find in their involvement an opportunity to express a concern for human values. Disablement allows some of them to be politically active in an area untouched by ideologies of the extreme right or left.

In contemplating what has been achieved it is all too easy to gloss over what remains to be done. Lord Snowdon's Working Party report prevents any complacency with its sharply worded attack on deficiencies in filling the financial, housing, vocational and leisure needs of the handicapped. But perhaps the most important facet of contemporary development is that the disabled are now beginning to speak for themselves, and are less and less willing to have their views and needs mediated by others — they are speaking to us directly, forcefully and with increasing political skill.

As to the future, there are several matters requiring urgent attention. The plight of mentally handicapped children in long-stay residential institutions needs to be considered as a matter of some priority. There are immense problems in raising the speech and reading standards of our deaf children. I would like to see an expansion of counselling and education services for parents with very young handicapped children. Post-school training for physically handicapped young people still needs to be improved even though the employment prospects in the immediate future do not seem very bright. We need to continue the present trend of educating and informing the public at all levels to remove the vestiges of prejudice and misunderstanding — my newspaper this morning reported a psychiatrist saying the deaf are usually paranoid!

In contrast there are many positive signs. The expansion and improvement of genetic counselling in conjunction with preventative measures (amniocentesis, the ultra-sound examination of the baby in the womb and the exciting potential of routine blood tests of pregnant women to detect the possible presence of malformations in the unborn child) will significantly reduce the incidence of handicapping conditions. Modern technology will make an even greater impact as such devices as the one which enables a blind baby to interpret his environment through audio signals become widely available. Access to public buildings for the disabled will continue to improve and new buildings will have the need of this group incorporated into their designs. There will be expansion in the number of specially adapted dwellings enabling the disabled to become part of their communities.

But the greatest gains will be made in the interpersonal area. Here the most significant and enduring advances are likely to be achieved through the accelerating trend of educating more and more handicapped children together with their non-handicapped peers.

Bibliography

Abrahams, P. (1973) The effect of deafness. *Hearing*, 27, 260-3.

Adams, G.R. and Cohen, A.S. (1974) Children's physical and interpersonal characteristics that effect student-teacher interactions. *J. Exp. Educ.*, 43, 1-5

Adelstein, A.M. *et al.* (1976) *Child Health, a Collection of Studies.* Studies on Medical and Population Subjects, no.31, Office of Population Censuses and Surveys, HMSO.

Adler, A. (1927) *The Practice and Theory of Individual Psychology.* New York, Harcourt Brace Jovanovich.

Anderson, E.M. (1973) *The Disabled Schoolchild.* London, Methuen.

Argyle, M. (ed.) (1973) *Social Encounters.* Harmondsworth, Penguin Books.

Argyle, M. (1975) *Bodily Communication.* London, Methuen.

Bagley, C. (1971) *The Social Psychology of the Child with Epilepsy.* London, Routledge.

Balbernie, R. (1973) The Cotswold experiment. *Community Schools Gazette*, 66, 522-64.

Barclay, A. and Vaught, G. (1964) Maternal estimates of future achievement in cerebral palsied children. *Amer. J. Ment. Defic.*, 64, 62-5.

Becker, H.S. (1963) *Outsiders: Studies in the Sociology of Deviance.* New York, Free Press.

Begab, M.J. (1968) *The Effects of Differences in Curricula and Experiences on Social Work Student Attitudes and Knowledge about Mental Retardation.* Bethesda, Maryland, US Department of Health, Education and Welfare, National Institute of Health.

Begab, M.J. and Richardson, S.A. (1975) *The Mentally Retarded and Society.* Baltimore University Press.

Belmont, J.M. (1971) Medical-behavioural research in retardation. In N.R. Ellis (ed.), *International Review of Research in Mental Retardation*, vol.5, New York, Academic Press, 1-81.

Berreman, J.V. (1954) Some implications of research in the social psychology of disability. *Exceptional Children*, 20, 347-50, 356-7.

Bettelheim, B. (1971) *The Children of the Dream*. St Albans, Paladin.

Bilsbury, C. and Bromley, D.B. (1974) Person perception in educationally subnormal children. Paper to Social Psychology Section of British Psychological Society Conference, 21 Sept. 1974.

Birenbaum, A. (1970) On managing a courtesy stigma. *J. of Health and Social Behaviour*, 11 (3), 196-206.

Birenbaum, A. (1971) The mentally retarded child in the home and the family cycle. *J. of Health and Social Behaviour*, 12, 55-65.

Blacketter-Simmonds, L.D.A. (1953) An investigation into the supposed differences existing between mongols and other mentally defective subjects with regard to certain psychological traits. *J. Ment. Sci.*, 99, 702-83.

Block, W.E. (1955) A study of somato-psychological relationships in cerebral palsied children. *Exceptional Children*, 22, 53-9, 77-83.

Blyth, W.A.L. (1968) The child in his culture. In *The Child and the Outside World*. Association for Special Education 29th Biennial Conference Report, 35-44.

Bogardus, E.S. (1925) Measuring social distances. *J. of Applied Sociol.*, Jan.-Feb., 216-22.

Boone, D.R. and Hartman, H. (1972) The benevolent over-reaction. *Clinical Pediatrics*, 11, 268-271.

Bowyer, L.R. and Gillies, J. (1972) The social and emotional adjustment of deaf and partially deaf children. *Brit. J. Educ. Psychol.*, 42, 303-8.

Braginsky, D.D. and Braginsky, B.M. (1972) The intelligent behaviour of mental retardates: a study of their manipulation of intelligence test scores. *J. of Personality*, 40, 558-63.

Bridge, E.M. (1949) *Epilepsy and Convulsive Disorders in Childhood*. New York, McGraw-Hill.

Bridgeland, M. (1971) *Pioneer Workers with Maladjusted Children*. London, Staples.

Bronfenbrenner, U. (1974) *Two Worlds of Childhood*. Harmondsworth, Penguin Books.

Brown, C. (1954) *My Left Foot*. London, Secker and Warburg.

Caldwell, B.M. and Gruze, S.B. (1960) A study of the adjustment of parents of institutionalized and non-institutionalized retarded children. *Am. J. Ment. Defic.*, 64, 845-61.

Chesler, M.A. (1965) Ethnocentrism and attitudes towards the physically disabled. *J. Pers. Soc. Psychol.*, 2, 877-82.

Clark, E.T. (1964) Children's perceptions of educable mentally retarded children. *Am. J. Ment. Defic.*, 68, 602-11.

Cleland, C.C. and Chambers, I.L. (1959) The effect of institutional tours on attitudes of high school seniors. *Am. J. Ment. Defic.*, 64, 124-30.

Clinard, M.B. (1968) *Sociology of Deviant Behaviour*. 3rd ed., New York, Holt, Rinehart.

Coard, B. (1971) *How the West Indian Child is Made Educationally Sub-normal in the British School System*. London, New Beacon.

Cook, J.J. (1963) Dimensional analysis of child-rearing attitudes of parents of handicapped children. *Am. J. Ment. Defic.*, 68, 354-61.

Cook, M. (1971) *Interpersonal Perceptions*. Harmondsworth, Penguin Books.

Court Report (1976) *Fit for the Future*. Report of the Committee on Child Health Services (Chairman, Professor S.D.M. Court), HMSO, Cmnd. 6684 (2 vols).

Coveney, P. (1967) *The Image of Childhood*. Harmondsworth, Penguin Books.

Cruickshank, W.M. (1952) A study of the relation of physical disability to social adjustment. *Am. J. of Occup. Therapy*, 3, 100-9, 141.

Dale, D.M.C. (1967) *Deaf Children at Home and at School*. University of London Press.

Darbyshire, J.O. (1970) The sociology of deafness. *Sound*, 4, 2-4.

Davis, F. (1964) Deviance disavowal: the management of strained interaction by the visibly handicapped. In H.S. Becker (ed.), *The Other Side*. New York, Free Press, 114-37.

Deacon, J.J. (1974) *Tongue Tied*. National Society for Mentally Handicapped Children.

de Mause, L. (ed.) (1976) *The History of Childhood*. London, Souvenir Press.

DES (1972) *Aspects of Special Education*. Education Survey no.17.

DES Statisitcs (1976) *Statistics of Education, 1975*. HMSO.

DES (2/75) *The Discovery of Children Requiring Special Education and the Assessment of their Needs*. HMSO.

Drimmer, F. (1976) *Very Special People: the Struggles, Loves and Triumphs of Human Oddities*. New York, Bantam.

Edgerton, R.B. (1963) A patient elite: ethnography in a hospital for the mentally retarded. *Am. J. Ment. Defic.*, 68, 372-85.

Efron, R.E. and Efron, H.U. (1967) Measurement of attitudes towards the retarded and an application with educators. *Am. J. Ment. Defic.*, 72, 100-7.

Ellis, H.J. (1974) Parental involvement in the decision to treat spina bifida cystica. *Brit. Med. J.*, 1, 369-72.

English, R.W. (1971) The application of personality theory to explain psychological reactions to physical disability. *Rehabilitation Research and Practice Review*, 3, 35-47.

Evans, K. (1962) *Sociometry and education*. London, Routledge.

Farber, B. (1959) *Effects of a Severely Retarded Child on Family Integration*. Soc. Res. in Child Dev. Monogr. no.24, 2.

Filstead, W.J. (1972) (ed.) *An Introduction to Deviance*, Chicago, Rand McNally.

Fishler, K.L., Donnell, G.N., Bergen, W.R. and Koch, R. (1972) Intellectual and personality development in children with galactosemia. *Pediatrics*, 50, 412-9.

Fishman, A. and Fishman, D.B. (1971) Emotional, cognitive and inter-personal confrontations among children with birth defect. *Child Psychiat. and Hum. Dev.*, 2, 92-101.

Fothergill, C. (1977) The development of a school for visually handicapped children in the light of educational thought and practice with special reference to the period 1944-74. M.Ed. Thesis, University of Liverpool.

Foulke, E. (1972) The personality of the blind: a non-valid concept. *New Outlook for the Blind*, 66, 33-7.

Fowler, H.W. (1975) *A Dictionary of Modern English Usage*. Oxford, Clarendon Press.

Fox, M.A. (1974) *They Get This Training but They Don't Know How You Feel*. Horsham, Sussex, National Foundation for Research into Crippling Diseases.

Freedman, J.L., Carlsmith, M. and Sears, D.O. (1970) *Social Psychology*. Englewood Cliffs, N.J., Prentice-Hall.

Gallignani's Literary Review (1821) Issue of 15 July.

Garlinghouse, J. and Sharp, L.J. (1968) The hemophilic child's self-concept and family stress in relation to bleeding episodes. *Nursing Research*, 17, 32-7.

Garrett, J.F. (1953) (ed.) *Psychological Aspects of Physical Disability*. US Dept. of Health, Education and Welfare, Office of Rehabilitation, no.210.

Gath, A. (1973) The school age siblings of mongol children. *Brit. J. Psychiat.*, 123, 161-7.

Gesell, A. and Amatruda, C.S. (1947) *Developmental Diagnosis: Normal and Abnormal Development*. New York, Harper and Hoeber.

Getzels, J.W. (1952) A psycho-social framework for the study of educational administration. *Harvard Educ. Rev.*, 22, 233-46.

Goffman, E. (1968) *Stigma*. Harmondsworth, Penguin Books.

Goffman, E. (1969) *Behaviour in Public Places*. New York, Free Press.

Goldberg, B., Lobb, H. and Kroll, H. (1975) Psychiatric problems of the deaf child. *Canad. Psychiat. Ass. J.*, 20, 75-83.

Goldin, G.J., Perry, S.L., Margolin, R.J., Stosky, B.A. and Foster, J.C. (1971) *The Rehabilitation of the Young Epileptic*. Lexington, Mass., Heath.

Goldman, R., and Shames, G.H. (1964) Comparison of the goals that parents of stutterers and parents of non-stutterers set for their children. *J. of Speech and Hearing Disorders*, 29, 381-9.

Goodman, M.E. (1972) *The Culture of Childhood*. Columbia, New York, Teachers College Press.

Gordon, G. (1966) *Role Theory and Illness*. New Haven, College and University Press.

Gordon, I. (1966) *Studying the Child in School.* New York, Wiley.

Gottfried, N.W. and Jones, R.L. (1970) Non-cognitive correlates of satisfaction in teaching the educable mentally retarded. *Education and Training of the Mentally Retarded,* 5, 37-43.

Gottlieb, J. and Davies, J.E. (1973) Social acceptability of E.M.R. children during overt behaviour interactions. *Am. J. Ment. Defic.,* 78, 141-3.

Gottlieb, J. (1975) Public, peer and professional attitudes towards mentally retarded persons. In Begab, M.J. and Richardson, S.A.(ed.) *The Mentally Retarded and Society,* Baltimore University Press.

Gottwald, H. (1970) *Public Awareness about Mental Retardation.* Research Monograph, Council for Exceptional Children.

Grailiker, B.V., Fishler, K. and Koch, R. (1962) Teenage Reaction to a Mentally Retarded Sibling. *Am. J. Ment. Defic.,* 66, 838-43.

Gregory, S. (1976) *The Deaf Child and His Family.* London, Allen and Unwin.

Griffiths, R.D. (1974) Personality Assessment. In P. Mittler (ed.) *The Psychological Assessment of Mental and Physical Handicap.* London, Tavistock.

Grinter, E.A. (1974) A study of self-concepts and self-acceptance of visually handicapped adolescents. Diploma Dissertation, University College of Swansea.

Haffter, C. (1968) The changeling: history and psychodynamics of attitudes to handicapped children in European folk-lore. *J. of History of Behavioural Sciences,* 4, 55-61.

Hall, E. (1970) The politics of special education. *Inequality in Education,* 3 and 4, 17-22.

Halstead, H. (1957) Abilities and behaviour of epileptic children. *J. Ment. Sci.,* 103, 28-47.

Hanks, J.R. and Hanks, L.M. (1948) The physically handicapped in certain non-occidental societies. *J. of Social Issues,* 4, 11-20.

Harrison, R.M. (1976) Epilepsy and stigma. *New Society,* 37, 726 (Sept.), 497-8.

Henderson, P. (1974) *Disability in Childhood and Youth.* Oxford University Press.

Heriot, J.J. and Schmickel, C.A. (1967) Maternal estimates of IQ in children evaluated for learning potential. *Am. J. Ment. Defic.,* 71, 920-4.

Hewett, S. (1970) *The Family and the Handicapped Child.* London, Allen and Unwin.

Hilgard, E.R. and Atkinson, R.C. (1967) *Introduction to Psychology.* 4th ed., New York, Harcourt Brace.

Hill, D. (1959) The difficult epileptic and his social environment. *Trans. Assoc. Indust. Med. Offrs.* 9, 46-50.

Himmelweit, H.T. and Swift, B. (1969) A model for the understanding of the school as a socialization agent. In Mussen, D.H., Langer, J. and Covington, M. (eds) *Trends and Issues in Development Psychology,* New York, Holt, Rinehart.

Holden, J. and Thomas, D.J. (1976) Social tactics and slow learners. *Special Education: Forward Trends*, 3, 2, 25-7.

Hollinshead, M.T. (1959) The social psychology of exceptional children (part 1). *Exceptional Children*, 26, 137-40.

Holt, K.S. (1957) The impact of mentally handicapped children upon their families. M.Ed. Thesis, University of Manchester.

Hunt, S. (1975) *Parents of the E.S.N.* Manchester, National Elfrida Rathbone Society.

Iano, R.P., Ayers, H.B., Hiller, J.F., McGehigan, and Walker, V.S. (1974) Sociometric status of retarded children in an integrative program. *Exceptional Children*, 40, 267-71.

Jacobs, J.F. and Pierce, M.L. (1968) The social position of retardates with brain-damage associated characteristcs. *Exceptional Children*, 34, 677-81.

Johnson, D.W. (1970) *The Social Psychology of Education*. New York, Grune and Stratton.

Jolly, H. (1971) New fronteers in paediatrics. *Trans. Med. Soc.*, 87, 14-22.

Jones, K. (1972) *A History of the Mental Health Services*. London, Routledge.

Jones, K. (1975) *Opening the Door: a Study of New Policies for the Mentally Handicapped*. London, Routledge.

Jones, R.L. (1974) The hierarchical structure of attitudes towards the exceptional. *Exceptional Children*, 40, 430-5.

Jones, R.L., Gottfried, N.W. and Owens, A. (1966) The social distance of the exceptional: a study at the high school level. *Exceptional Children*, 32, 551-6.

Jordan, J.E. and Friesen, E.W. (1969) Attitudes of rehabilitation personnel towards physically disabled persons in Colombia, Peru and in the United States. *J. Soc. Psychol.*, 78, 151-61.

Kates, S.L. and Kates, F.F. (1965) Social and non-social concepts of deaf and hearing pupils. *J. Abnorm. Psychol.*, 70, 214-7.

Katz, A.H. (1961) *Parents of the Handicapped*. Springfield, Ill., Thomas.

Kelly, G.A. (1955) *The Psychology of Personal Constructs*. New York, Norton.

Kew, S. (1975) *Handicap and Family Crisis*. London, Pitman.

Kinn, W.T. (1964) Self-report of physically handicapped and non-handicapped children. *Dissertation Abstracts*, 24, 12, 5196-7.

Kleck, R. (1966) Emotional arousal in interactions with stigmatized persons. *Psychol. Reports*, 19, 1226.

Klein, J. (1965) *Samples from English Cultures*. London, Routledge.

Klineberg, O. (1968) Prejudice — the concept. In D.L. Sills (ed.), *International Encyclopedia of the Social Sciences*. New York, Macmillan.

Krebs, D.L. (1970) Altruism — an examination of the concept and a review of the literature. *Psychol. Bulletin*, 73, 4, 258-302.

Kretschmer, E. (1926) *Physique and Character*. New York, Harcourt Brace Jovanovich.

Kurtz, R. (1964) Implications of recent sociological research in mental retardation. *Am. J. Ment. Defic.*, 69, 506-10.

154   *The Social Psychology of Childhood Disability*

Laing, A. (1972) Group structure in retarded adolescents. *Am. J. Ment. Defic.*, 76, 481-90.

Langan, W. (1970) Visual perceptual difficulties. In P. Mittler (ed.), *The Psychological Assessment of Mental and Physical Handicaps*, London, Methuen.

Lawrence, E.A. and Winschel, J.A. (1973) Self-concept and the retarded — research and issues. *Exceptional Children*, 39, 310-7.

Lemert, E.M. (1967) *Human Deviance, Social Problems and Social Control.* Englewood Cliffs, N.J., Prentice-Hall.

Levine, S. (1970) A proposed conceptual framework for special education. In Meisgeier, C.H. and King, J.D. (ed.) *The Process of Special Education Administration.* Scranton, Pennsylvania, National Text Book Co.

Lewis, T. (1971) The self-concepts of adolescent educationally subnormal boys. M.Sc. Dissertation, University of Bradford.

Lindzey, G. and Aronson, E. (1969) *The Handbook of Social Psychology.* 2nd ed., Reading, Mass., Addison-Wesley.

Loudon, J.B. (1970) Teasing and socialization on Tristan da Cunha. In P. Mayer (ed.), *Socialization; the Approach from Social Anthropology.* London, Tavistock.

Love, H.D. (1970) *Parental Attitudes towards Exceptional Children.* Springfield, Ill., Thomas.

Lowenfeld, B. (1971) *Our Blind Children.* 3rd ed., Springfield, Ill., Thomas.

Lowenfeld, B. (1974) (ed.) *The Visually Handicapped Child in School.* London, Constable.

Lukoff, I.F., Cohen, O. *et al.* (1972) *Attitudes towards Blind Persons.* New York, American Foundation for the Blind.

Lumsden, J. (1966) What is special about special education? *International Conference Report*, Association for Special Education.

Luria, A.R. (1963) *The Mentally Retarded Child.* Oxford, Pergamon.

MacAndrews, C. and Edgerton, R. (1966) On the possibility of friendship. *Am. J. Ment. Defic.*, 70, 612-21.

McDaniel, J.W. (1969) *Physical Disability and Human Behaviour.* New York, Pergamon.

McMaster, J.M. (1973) *Towards an Educational Theory for the Mentally Handicapped.* London, Edward Arnold.

Mallenby, T. (1973) A note on the self-acceptance of institutionalized mentally retarded children. *J. Genet. Psychol.*, 123, 171-2.

Mallenby, T. (1974) Personal Space; projective and direct measures with institutionalized mentally retarded children. *J. Personality Assessment*, 38, 28-31.

Mannoni, M. (1973) *The Retarded Child and the Mother.* London, Tavistock.

Marge, D.K. (1966) The social status of speech handicapped children. *J. of Speech and Hearing Research*, 9, 165-77.

Martino, M.S., and Newman, M.B. (1974) Siblings of retarded children: a population at risk. *Child Psychol. and Hum. Dev.*, 4, 168-77.

Mayer, P. (1970) (ed.) *Socialization; the Approach from Social Anthropology*. London, Tavistock.

Mendelsohn, H. (1954) A sociological approach to certain aspects of mental deficiency. *Am. J. Ment. Defic.*, 58, 506-10.

Mercer, J. (1971) Socio-cultural factors in labelling mentally retardates. *Peabody J. of Education*, 48, 188-203.

Mercer, J. (1972) Who is normal? Two perspectives on mild mental retardation. In E.G. Jaco (ed.), *Patients, Physicians and Illness*. New York, Free Press.

Merton, R. (1957) *Social Theory and Social Structure*. Glencoe, Ill., Free Press.

Meyerson, L. (1955) Somatopsychology of Physical Disability. In W.M. Cruickshank (ed.), *Psychology of Exceptional Children and Youth*. Englewood Cliffs, N.J., Prentice-Hall.

Miller, E.J. and Gwynne, G.V. (1974) *A Life Apart*. London, Tavistock.

Minde, K.K., Hackett, J.D.,Killon, D. and Silver, S. (1972) How they grow up: 41 physically handicapped children and their families. *Am. J. Psychiat.*, 128, 1554-60.

Minton, H.G. (1974) *Blind Man's Buff*. London, Elek.

Moss, P. and Silver, O. (1972) *Mentally Handicapped School Children and Their Families*. Liverpool Education Department and London University Child Development Unit.

Munday, D. (1976) *Dorcas: Opportunity Not Pity*. Produced for PHAB (Physically Handicapped and Able Bodied) by Midas Books, Tunbridge Wells.

Murphy, E.A. (1972) The normal and the perils of the sylleptic argument. *Perspect. Biol. Med.*, 15, 566-82.

Murphy, E.A. (1973) The normal. *Am. J. Epidemiol.*, 98, 403-11.

Myers, S.O. (1975) *Condover Hall School: Where Are They Now? A Follow-up Study of 314 Multi-handicapped Blind People*. Royal National Institute for the Blind, London.

Myklebust, H.R. (1964) *The Psychology of Deafness*. New York, Grune and Stratton.

Nakauchi, M. (1972) Analysis of personality formation of children affected with Down's syndrome. *Psychiatrica et Neurologica Japonica*, 74, 183-4 (English abstract).

Nash, R. (1973) *Classrooms Observed*. London, Routledge.

National Union of Students (1976) *The Disabled Student*. Action Research for the Crippled Child and the National Union of Students.

Neer, W.L., Foster, D.A. *et al.* (1973) Socio-economic bias in the diagnosis of mental retardation. *Exceptional Children*, 40, 38-9.

Neuhaus, M. (1969) Parental attitudes and the emotional adjustment of deaf children. *Exceptional Children*, 35, 721-7.

Nightingale, B. (1973) *Charities*. London, Allen Lane.

Noonan, J.R., Barry, J.R. and Davis, H.C. (1970) Personality deter-
minants in attitudes towards visible disablity. *J. of Personality*, 38, 1-15.

Nuffield, J.A. (1961) Neuro-physiology and behaviour disorders in epileptic children. *J. Ment. Sci.*, 107, 348-88.

Nussbaum, J. (1962) An investigation of the relationship between self-
concept, mothers' concept and the reality orientation of adolescents with
cerebral palsy. *Dissertation Abstracts*, 22, 12, 4410-1.

Olch, D. (1971) Personality characteristics of haemophiliacs. *J. of Personality Assessment*, 35, 72-9.

Opie, I. and Opie, P. (1959) *The Lore and Language of Schoolchildren*.
Oxford University Press.

Park, C.C. (1972) *The Siege*. Harmondsworth, Penguin Books.

Parsons, T. (1951) *The Social System*. Glencoe, Ill., Free Press.

Pearson, G. (1975) *The Deviant Imagination*. London, Macmillan.

Phelps, W.M. (1948) Characteristic psychological variations in cerebral
palsy. *The Nervous Child*, 1, 73-4.

Pilkington, T.L. (1973) Public and professional attitudes to mental
handicap. *Public Health London*, 87, 61-6.

Pilling, D. (1973) *The Child with a Chronic Medical Problem*. National
Children's Bureau, National Foundation for Educational Research.

Pinkerton, P. and Weaver, C.M. (1970) Childhood asthma. In O.W. Hill
(ed.), *Modern Trends in Psychosomatic Medicine*, vol.2, London,
Butterworths.

Pond, D.A. (1952) Psychiatric aspects of epilepsy in children. *J. Ment. Sci.*,
98, 404-10.

Poznanski, E.O. (1973) Emotional issues in raising handicapped children.
Rehabilitation Literature, 34, 322-6.

Pringle, M.L.K. (1964) *The Emotional and Social Adjustment of Blind
Children*. National Foundation for Educational Research.

Pritchard, D.G. (1963) *Education and the Handicapped, 1760-1960*.
London, Routledge.

Pritchard, D.G. (1973) Special Education. In J. Stroud (ed.), *Services for
Children and their Families*. London, Pergamon.

Pritchard, D.G. (1973) 'Special Education', In J. Stroud (ed.), *Services for
children and their families*. London, Pergamon.

Rackham, K. (1975) The role of boarding schools in the treatment of
children with recurrent disabling disorders. *Child Care, Health and
Development*, 1, 19-27.

Rau, D.N. (1967) Parental attitudes of the educable mentally retarded
child as related to school achievement. *Dissertation Abstracts*, 28,
1350-1.

Reed, M. (1970) Deaf and partially hearing children. In P. Mittler (ed.),
The Psychological Assessment of Mental and Physical Handicaps.
London, Methuen.

Reynolds, M.C. (1960) The social psychology of exceptional children. *Exceptional Children*, 26, 243-7.

Richardson, S.A. (1968) The effects of physical disability on the socialization of a child. In D.A. Goslin (ed.), *Handbook of Socialization Theory and Research*. Chicago, Rand McNally.

Richardson, S.A. (1970) Age and sex differences in values towards physical handicap. *J. of Health and Social Behaviour*, 11, 207-14.

Richardson, S.A., Goodman, N., Hastorf, A. and Dornbusch, S.M. (1961) Cultural uniformity in reactions to physical disabilities. *Am. Sociol. Rev.*, 26, 241-7.

Richardson, S.A., Ronald, L. and Kleck, R.E. (1974) The social status of handicapped and non-handicapped boys in a camp setting. *J. Spe. Educ.*, 8, 143-52.

Roith, A.I. (1963) The myth of parental attitudes. *J. Ment. Subnormality*, 9, 51-4.

Ross, A.O. (1964) *The Exceptional Child in the Family*. New York, Grune and Stratton.

Rucker, C.N., Howe, C.E. and Snider, B. (1969) The participation of retarded children in junior high academic and non-academic regular classes. *Exceptional Children*, 36, 617-23.

Rutter, M.L., Graham, P.J. and Yule, W. (1970) *A Neuro-psychiatric Study in Childhood*. London, Heinemann Medical.

Rutter, M., Tizard, J. and Whitmore, K. (1970) *Education, Health and Behaviour*. London, Longman.

Sahakian, W.S. (1974) *Systematic Social Psychology*. New York, Chandler.

Sarnoff, I., Katz, D. and McClintock, C. (1970) Attitude change procedures and motivating patterns. In *Understanding Society*, Open University Press and Macmillan.

Schilder, P. (1950) *The Image and Appearance of the Human Body*. New York, Wiley.

Scott, R.A. (1968) The socialization of blind children. In D.A. Goslin (ed.), *Handbook of Socialization Theory and Research*. Chicago, Rand McNally, 1025-45.

Scott, R.A. (1969) *The Making of Blind Men*. New York, Russell Sage Foundation.

Scott, R.A. (1970) The construction of conceptions of stigma by professional experts. In J.D. Douglas (ed.), *Deviancy and Respectability*. New York, Basic Books.

Seitz, S. and Terdal, L. (1972) A modelling approach to changing parent-child interaction. *Mental Retardation*, 10, 39-43.

Semmel, M.L. and Dickson, S. (1966) Connotative reactions of college students to disability labels. *Exceptional Children*, 32, 442-50.

Sereny, G. (1972) Paul Tessier. *Daily Telegraph Magazine*, 422, 19-28.

Sharples, D. and Thomas, D.J. (1969) The perceived prestige of normal and special education teachers. *Exceptional Children*, 35, 473-9.

158 *The Social Psychology of Childhood Disability*

Shakespeare, R. (1975) *The Psychology of Handicap*. London, Methuen.
Shears, L.M. and Jensema, C.J. (1969) Social acceptability of anomalous persons. *Exceptional Children*, 36, 91-6.
Sheldon, W.H. and Stevens, S.S. (1942) *Varieties of Temperament*. New York, Harper and Row.
Shepherd, B.D. (1973) Parental potential. *Volta Review*, 75, 220-4.
Shere, M.O. (1956) Socio-emotional factors in families of the twin with cerebral palsy. *Exceptional Children*, 22, 197-9, 206-8.
Sheridan, M. (1973) *The Handicapped Child and His Home*. National Children's Home.
Shipman, M. (1968) *The Sociology of the School*. London, Longman.
Silverstein, A.B. (1964) An empirical test of the mongoloid stereotype. *Am. J. Ment. Defic.*, 68, 493-7.
Smits, S.J. (1964) Reactions of self and others to the obviousness and severity of physical disablity. *Dissertation Abstracts*, 25, 2, 1324-5.
Snow, C.P. (1968) *Varieties of Men*. London, Macmillan.
Snowdon Working Party (2976) *Integrating the Disabled*. Report of the Snowdon Working Party, National Fund for Research into Crippling Disease.
Somers, V.C. (1944) *The Influence of Parental Attitudes on the Personality Development of the Adolescent Blind*. American Foundation for the Blind.
Spock, B. (1968) *Baby and Child Care*. London, New English Library.
Staples, R. (1971) Towards a sociology of the black family. *J. of Marriage and the Family*, 35, 119-38.
Swift, C.R., Seidman, F. and Stein, H. (1967) Adjustment problems of juvenile diabetics. *Psychosomatic Medicine*, 29, 555-71.
Tajfel, H. (1969) Cognitive aspects of prejudice. *J. Biosoc. Sci.*, suppl. 1, 173-91.
Tenny, J. (1953) The minority status of the handicapped. *Exceptional Children*, 19, 260-4.
Tew, B., Laurence, K.M. and Samuel, P. (1974) Parental estimates of the intelligence of their physically handicapped child. *Devel. Med. Child Neurol.*, 16, 494-500.
Thomas, J.B. (1971) A study of the self-concepts of pupils in their final year at a streamed junior school. M.Ed. Thesis, University of Wales.
Thomas, E.C. and Yamamoto, K. (1970) Emotionally disturbed school-children and their school related perceptions. *Exceptional Children*, 36, 623-4.
Thomas E.J. (1966) The problem of disability from the perspective of role theory. *J. of Health and Human Behaviour*, 7, 2-13.
Thomas K. (1977) The place of laughter in Tudor and Stuart England. *The Times Literary Supplement* (Jan.21), 77-81.
Titmuss, R.M. (1970) *The Gift Relationship: From Human Blood to Social Policy*. London, Allen and Unwin.

Tizard, B. (1962) The personality of epileptics: a discussion of the evidence. *Psychol. Bulletin*, 59, 3, 196-210.

Tizard, J. (1964) *Community Services for the Mentally Handicapped.* London, Oxford University Press.

Tizard, J. and Grad, J.C. (1961) *The Mentally Handicapped and Their Families.* London, Oxford University Press.

Tizard, J. and Tizard, B. (1974) The institution as an environment for development. In M.P.M. Richards (ed.), *The Integration of the Child into a Social World.* Cambridge University Press, 137-52.

Tobin, M.J. (1972) Attitudes of non-specialist teachers towards visually handicapped pupils. *Teacher of the Blind*, 60, 60-4.

Townsend, P. (1973) The disabled in society. In D.M. Boswell and J.M. Wingrove (eds), *The Handicapped Person in the Community.* London, Tavistock.

Trippe, M.W. (1959) The social psychology of exceptional children. *Exceptional Children*, 26, 171-5, 188.

Tuckey, R. and Tuckey, L. (1974) Handicapped school leavers. *Secondary Education*, 4, 132-4.

Voysey, M. (1972) Impression management by parents of disabled children. *J. of Health and Social Behaviour*, 13, 80-9.

Voysey, M. (1975) *A Constant Burden.* London, Routledge.

Wachs, D.T. (1966) Personality testing and the handicapped. *J. of Proj. Tech. and Person. Assment*, 30, 339-55.

Walters, J. and Stinnett, N. (1971) Parent-child relationships: a decade review of research. *J. of Marriage and the Family*, 31, 70-111.

Wechsler, D. (1974) *Wechsler Intelligence Scale for Children — Revised.* New York, The Psychological Corporation.

Weiss, D. and Weinstein, E. (1968) Interpersonal tactics among the mentally retarded. *Am. J. Ment. Defic.*, 72, 653-61.

White, M.A. and Charry, J. (1966) (eds) *School Disorder, Intelligence and Social Class.* Columbia, New York, Teachers College Press.

Whitmore, K. (1975) What do we mean by maladjustment? Then why don't we say so! In A.F. Laing (ed.), *Trends in the Education of Children with Special Learning Needs.* Faculty of Education, University College of Swansea.

Wilkes, J. (1972) Making pathways in the brain. *Observer Magazine* (10 Dec.).

Willey, N.R. and McCandless, B.R. (1973) Social stereotypes of normal, E.M.R. and orthopaedically handicapped children. *J. of Special Educ.*, 7, 283-8.

Willower, D. (1970) Special education: organization and administration. *Exceptional Children*, 36, 591-4.

Wolfensberger, W. and Kurtz, R.A. (1971) Measurement of parents' perceptions of their children's development. *Genet. Psychol. Monogr.*, 83, 3-92.

Woolfe, R. (1977) The definition of maladjustment. M.Ed. Thesis, University College of Wales, Cardiff.

Wright, B.A. (1960) *Physical Disability: a Psychological Approach*. New York, Harper.

Wylie, R.C. (1961) *The Self-Concept*. Lincoln, University of Nebraska Press.

Younghusband, E. (1970) (ed.), *Living with Handicap*. London, Longman, for the National Children's Bureau.

Yuker, H.E., Block, J.R. and Young. J.H. (1966) *The Measurement of Attitudes Towards Disabled Persons*. Human Resources Study no.7. Resources Foundation.

Yuker, H.E., Block, J.R. and Younng, J.H. (1966) *The Measurement of of Attitudes Towards Disabled Persons*. Human Resource Study no.7. Albertson, N.Y., Human Resources Foundation.

Zigler, E. (1966) Mental Retardation: Current Issues and Approaches. In L. and M. Hoffman (eds), *Review of Child Development Research*. New York, Russell Sage Foundation.

Index